CENTRAL BIRMINGHAM

HISTORY TOUR

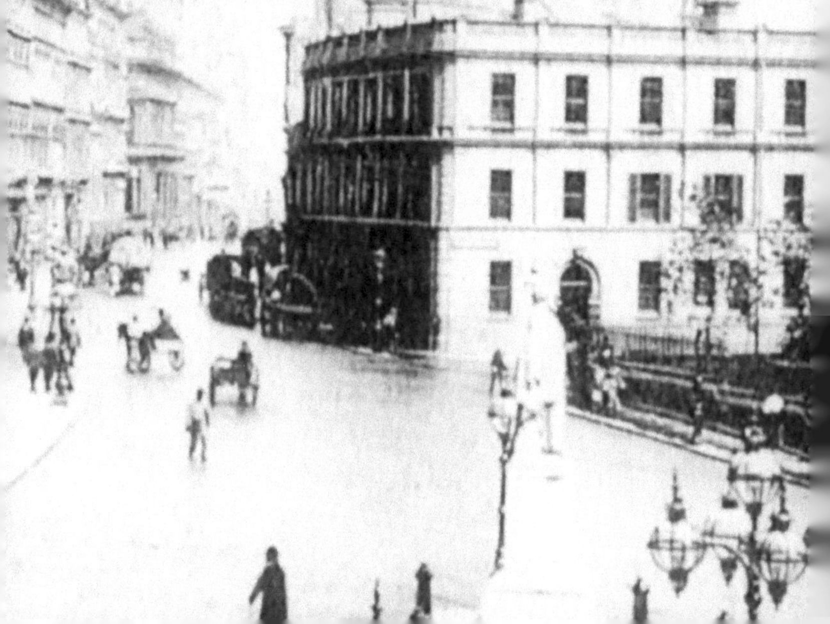

Technical help provided by daughter Rosemary and grandson John Fox,
is deeply appreciated by the author.

First published 2016

Amberley Publishing
The Hill, Stroud,
Gloucestershire, GL5 4EP
www.amberley-books.com

Copyright © Eric Armstrong, 2016
Map contains Ordnance Survey data
© Crown copyright and database right
[2016]

The right of Eric Armstrong to be
identified as the Author of this work
has been asserted in accordance with
the Copyrights, Designs and Patents
Act 1988.

ISBN 978 1 4456 5763 9 (print)
ISBN 978 1 4456 5764 6 (ebook)

British Library Cataloguing in
Publication Data.
A catalogue record for this book is
available from the British Library.

Typesetting by Amberley Publishing.
Printed in Great Britain.

Appointed GPSR EU Representative:
Easy Access System Europe Oü,
16879218
Address: Mustamäe tee 50, 10621,
Tallinn, Estonia
Contact Details: gpsr.requests@
easproject.com, +358 40 500 3575

INTRODUCTION

At the start of the eighteenth century, Birmingham was a small market town like many others. By the middle of the century, many local folk were busy in small workshops manufacturing a wide variety of metal goods, from nails to pots and pans, ladles to metal buttons. The skills of the smiths who turned out guns and those of master craftsmen in the jewellery trade became legendary. This small town had developed into a major, rapidly growing member of the Industrial Revolution.

Prominent among the 'movers and shakers' of this richly inventive period were Boulton, Watt and Murdoch: one highly capable businessman and two Scots – top-notch engineers and inventors. These men created a factory in the neighbouring locality of Soho, which opened in 1762 and became well known worldwide.

Throughout the nineteenth century, the now industrial town continued to grow, achieving parliamentary borough status in 1838 and, to the citizens' great delight, city status in 1888. In 1911 the new city, in keeping with the city's motto 'Forward', grew dramatically by taking in neighbours as city suburbs, such as Handsworth, Aston, Erdington, Yardley, King's Norton and Northfield. This brought the population up to nearly a million. By this time, the city was often called the 'workshop of the world' and a 'city of a thousand trades' – both popular accolades.

Various titans of industry were well established before the First World War began in 1914, including Averys, Austin, BSA, Cadbury, Elkington, GEC, GKN, Lucas, Wolseley.

So, from its small town beginnings, Birmingham had developed into England's second major industrial city. However, this massive success had its drawbacks. One perennial question ran: 'What shall we do about the city centre?' Many of the key central routes have retained their medieval road layout and buildings, a network that included the route from the broad south to the now iconic Bull Ring market place area, which linked to High Street, Bull Street, and New Street – just some of the old to be made new. These roads, along with others in in the city centre, are shown in the postcard illustrations featured throughout this book. While many of the cards date from the 1920s and 1930s, quite a few are a century old.

By 1901, acres of slums in Birmingham had been demolished and the politician Joseph Chamberlain, a man of drive and vision, saw his dream of Corporation Street made real.

By way of rounding off the above history notes, attention is drawn to Birmingham's coat of arms. The armorial bearings of the long gone de Bermingham family enhance the shield. When the town was awarded city status, two figures were allowed to be added by choice. So we now have a smith in working gear, resting his hammer on an anvil, representing industry, and a lady in flowing clothes holding a large palette and brush, symbolic of art.

Despite the wane of manufacturing in recent times, the city is still probably widely regarded as being an industrial rather than artistic city. However, Birmingham has been strong in the arts since early in the nineteenth century, and during the last fifty years art and industry together have achieved marked success in the city centre. We have witnessed the rejuvenation of the canal system, new seats of learning, sport and entertainment, and the development of Centenary Square – 'Forward' remains the watchword.

KEY

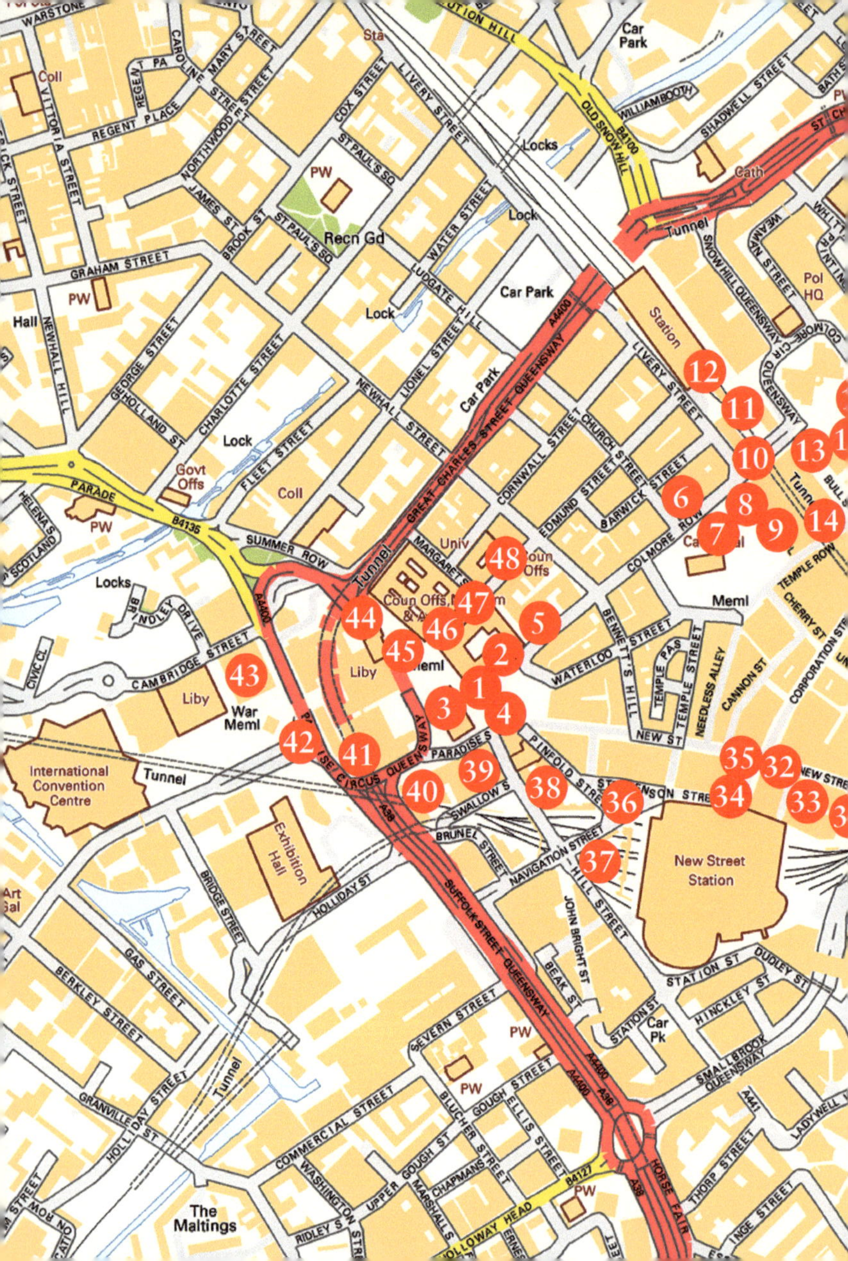

WARSTONE
Coll
VITTORIA STREET
CK STREET
Hall
NEWHALL HILL
HELENA ST
SCOTLAND
PARADE
B4136
PW
Locks
BINDLEY DRIVE
CAMBRIDGE STREET
Liby
War Meml
42
International Convention Centre
Tunnel
43
CIVIC CL
Art Gal
BERKLEY STREET
GAS STREET
BRIDGE STREET
Tunnel
GRANVILLE STREET
HOLLIDAY STREET
The Maltings
CAROLINE STREET
REGENT PA
REGENT PLACE
GRAHAM STREET
PW
GEORGE STREET
HOLLAND ST
CHARLOTTE STREET
Govt Offs
FLEET STREET
Lock
Coll
SUMMER ROW
A4400
Tunnel
44
45
Liby
Meml
41
PARADISE CIRCUS
Tunnel
Exhibition Hall
HOLLIDAY ST
COMMERCIAL STREET
WASHINGTON STREET
RIDLEY S
NORTHWOOD STREET
JAMES ST
BROOK ST
MARY STREET
ST PAUL'S SQ
PW
Recn Gd
ST PAUL'S SQ
Lock
NEWHALL STREET
Lock
MARGARET S
Univ
Coun Offs, Mus & Art
46
48
47
5
2
1
3
4
SWALLOW S
BRUNEL STREET
SUFFOLK STREET QUEENSWAY
SEVERN STREET
GOUGH STREET
UPPER GOUGH ST
MARSHALL S
CHAPMANS
HOLLOWAY HEAD
COX STREET
LIVERY STREET
Sta
LUDGATE HILL
WATER STREET
Lock
Lock
LIONEL STREET
Car Park
GREAT CHARLES STREET QUEENSWAY
A4400
Car Park
CORNWALL STREET
EDMUND STREET
Coun Offs
39
40
PARADISE S
QUEENSWAY
A38
PINFOLD STREET
38
NAVIGATION STREET
STEPHENSON STRE
36
37
BLUCHER STREET
ELLIS STREET
PW
A4400
A38
HORSE FAIR
PW
B4127
OLD SNOW HILL
WILLIAM BOOTH
B4100
Locks
Tunnel
Station
CHURCH STREET
BARWICK STREET
COLMORE ROW
12
11
10
6
7
8
9
Cath
Meml
Waterloo
BENNETT'S HILL
TEMPLE PAS
TEMPLE STREET
TEMPLE ROW
Meml
NEW ST
CANNON ST
NEEDLESS ALLEY
CHERRY ST
CORPORATION
35
32
34
33
New Street
Station
STATION ST
JOHN BRIGHT ST
BEAK ST
HILL STREET
Car Pk
STATION ST
DUDLEY ST
HINCKLEY ST
SMALLBROOK QUEENSWAY
THORP STREET
INGE STREET
SHADWELL STREET
SNOW HILL QUEENSWAY
Car Park
BATH
ST CH
Pol HQ
QUEENSWAY
Cath
Tunnel
13
14
1
BULL S
Car Offs
COLMORE CIR QUEENSWAY
WHITT
PINTIN
WEAM
NEW STREET
A441
LADYWELL

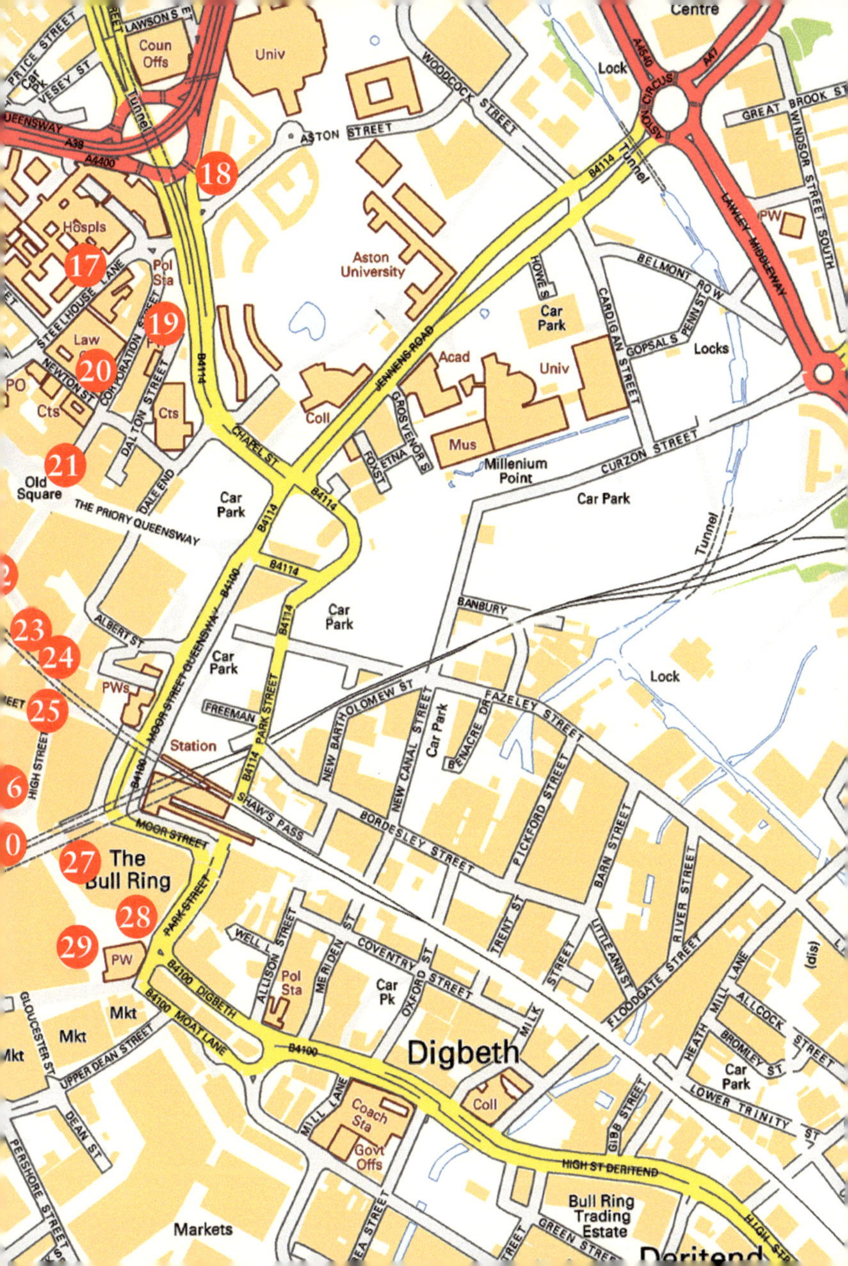

Centre
PRICE STREET
Coun Offs
Univ
WOODCOCK STREET
Lock
ASTON CIRCUS
A4540
A47
GREAT BROOK ST
VESEY ST
QUEENSWAY
A38
A4400
18
ASTON STREET
Tunnel
B4114
LAWLEY MIDDLEWAY
WINDSOR STREET SOUTH
PW
Hospls
17
STEELHOUSE LANE
Pol Sta
Aston University
JENNENS ROAD
Car Park
Acad
HOWE S
BELMONT ROW
PENN ST
GOPSAL S
CARDIGAN STREET
Locks
19
Law
20
CORPORATION STREET
NEWTON ST
DALTON STREET
Cts
Cts
CHAPEL ST
Coll
Univ
Mus
FOXST
GROSVENOR S
ETNA
Millenium Point
CURZON STREET
PO
21
Old Square
THE PRIORY QUEENSWAY
DALE END
Car Park
B4114
B4114
Car Park
Car Park
Tunnel
2
BANBURY
23
ALBERT ST
B4400
MOOR STREET QUEENSWAY
24
Car Park
Lock
PWs
FAZELEY STREET
25
FREEMAN
PARK STREET
B4114
New Canal Street
Car Park
BENACRE DR
PICKFORD STREET
BARN STREET
6
HIGH STREET
Station
NEW BARTHOLOMEW ST
0
MOOR STREET
SHAW'S PASS
BORDESLEY STREET
TRENT ST
LITTLE ANN ST
FLOODGATE STREET
RIVER STREET
27
The Bull Ring
PARK STREET
28
WELL L
ALLISON STREET
MERIDEN ST
OXFORD ST
COVENTRY STREET
MILK
HEATH MILL LANE
ALLCOCK STREET
BROMLEY ST
29
PW
B4100 DIGBETH
Pol Sta
Car Pk
GIBB STREET
GLOUCESTER ST
B4100 MOAT LANE
Car Park
Mkt
Mkt
UPPER DEAN STREET
B4100
Digbeth
LOWER TRINITY
Mkt
DEAN ST
MILL LANE
Coach Sta
Govt Offs
Coll
HIGH ST DERITEND
PERSHORE STREET
REA STREET
Markets
Bull Ring Trading Estate
GREEN STREET
HIGH
Deritend

1. VICTORIA SQUARE

Being partly bordered by three 'heritage buildings', Victoria Square is admirably placed to be the starting point for a walk – alone, or in a group. During recent years, the mix of passers-by has become increasingly, and interestingly, more cosmopolitan.

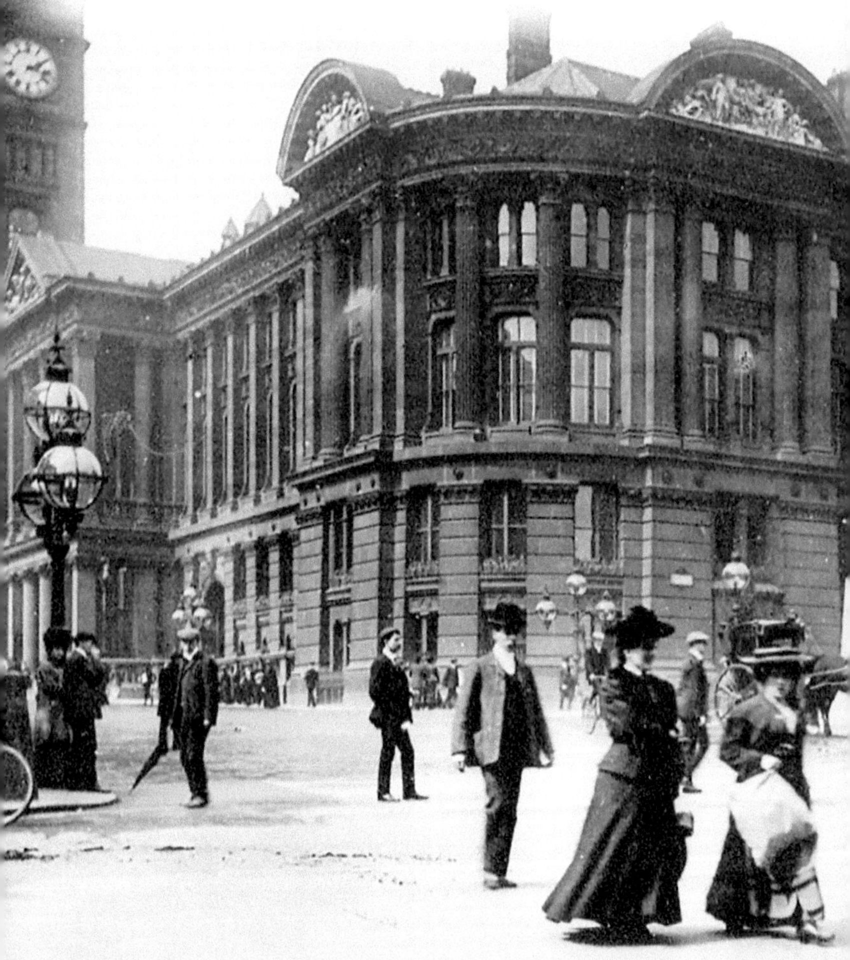

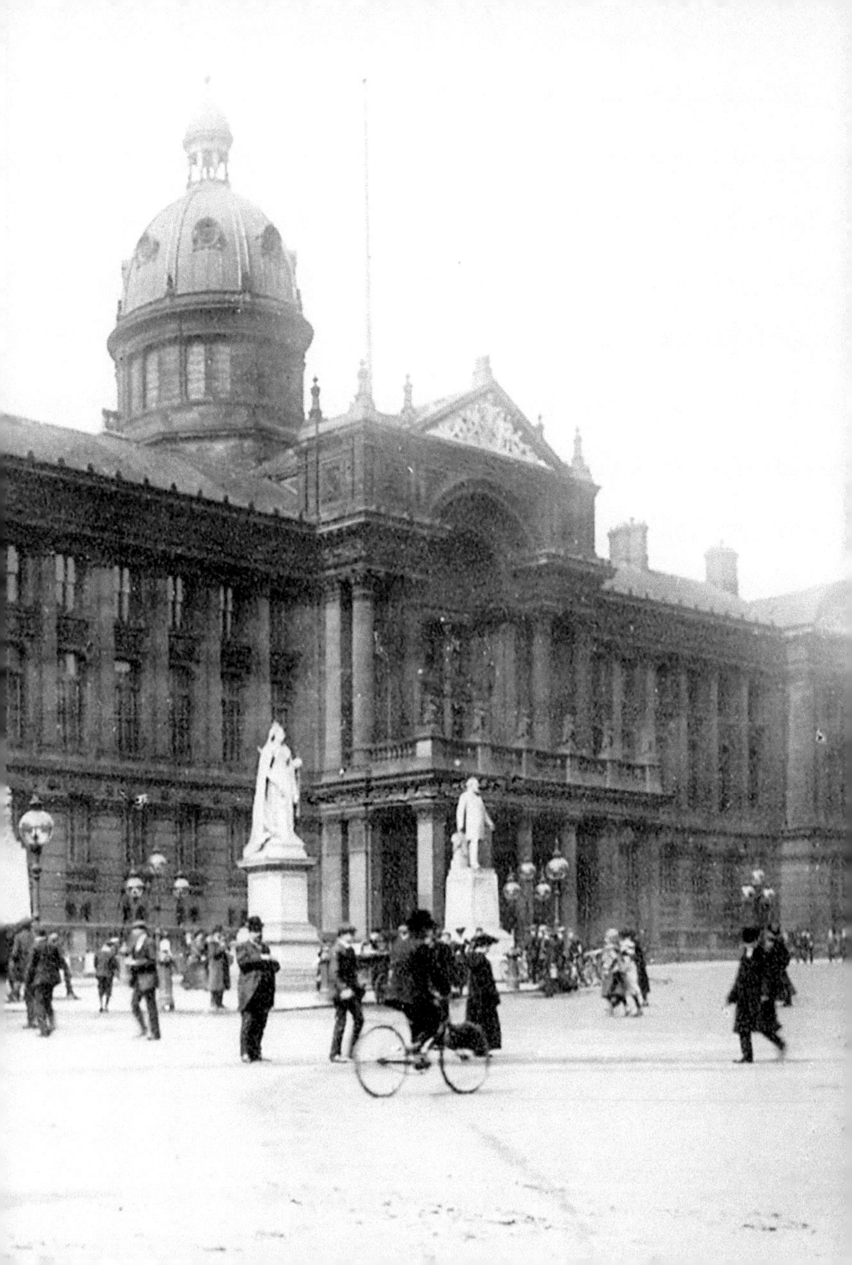

2. COUNCIL HOUSE

This heritage building, the powerhouse of democratic local government, was opened in 1879. The social reforms successfully achieved owed much to the radical politician Joseph Chamberlain, who served as mayor from 1873 to 1876, setting in motion major reforms in housing, commercial buildings, public health, and education. Much admired by Birmingham people, 'Old Joe' became the first chancellor of the University of Birmingham. Inside, reached by a grand staircase, three ornately decorated rooms with elliptical ceilings were available for use. The inset image shows one of these – the banqueting room.

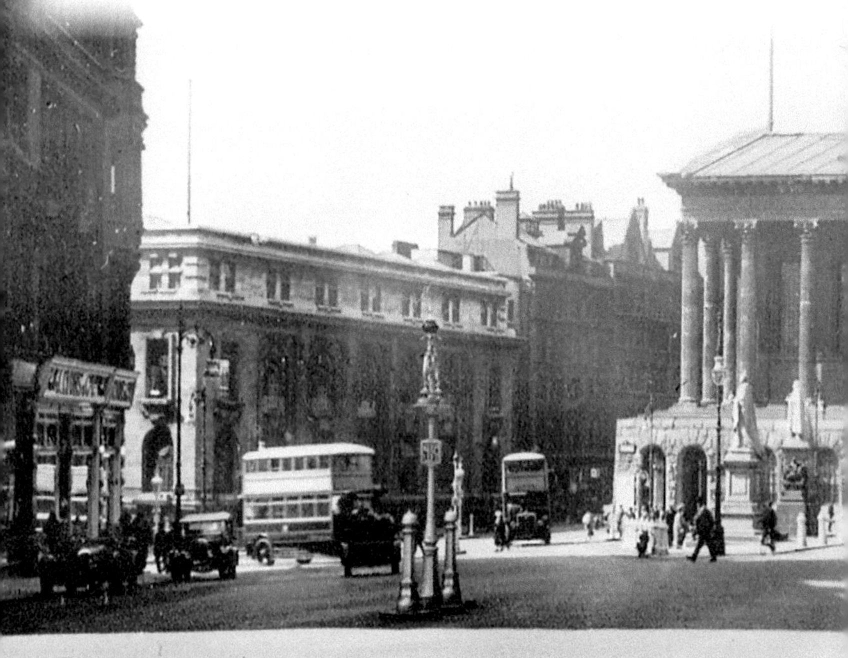

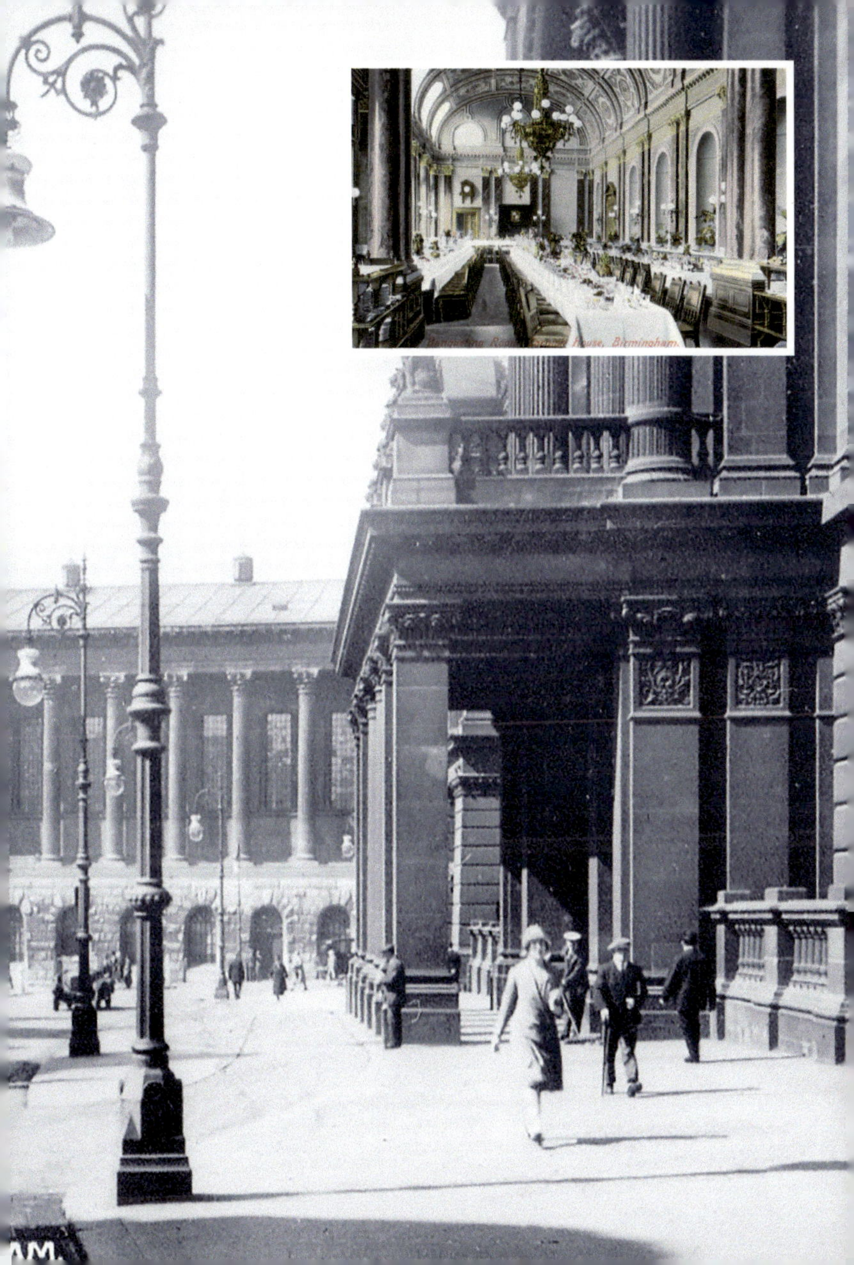
Banqueting Room, Council House, Birmingham.

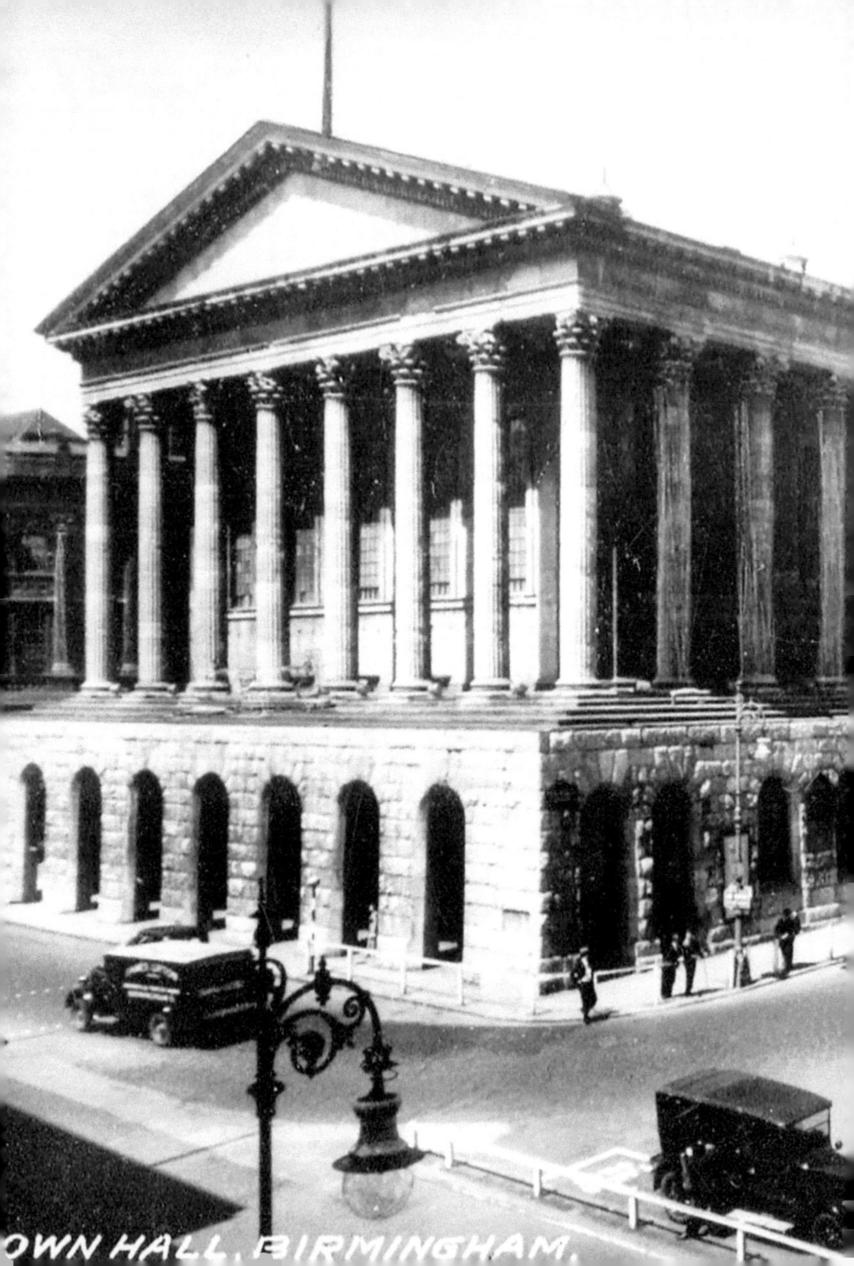
OWN HALL, BIRMINGHAM.

3. TOWN HALL

Anglesey marble clads the brick of which the Town Hall (another heritage building) is formed. The building's design was based on a Roman temple. Its origins date back to the 1830s, but later changes to the building enabled the public to attend a wider range of activities: music of all kinds, political debates, and fundraising events. From the outset, the city was able to attract top-notch musicians, including Felix Mendelssohn and Sir John Barbirolli. Then, in 1919, the council took the bold step to subsidise the City of Birmingham's orchestra with ratepayer's money. The CBSO, as it became known, attracted top conductors to flourish their batons, for example, Sir Adrian Boult and Sir Simon Rattle.

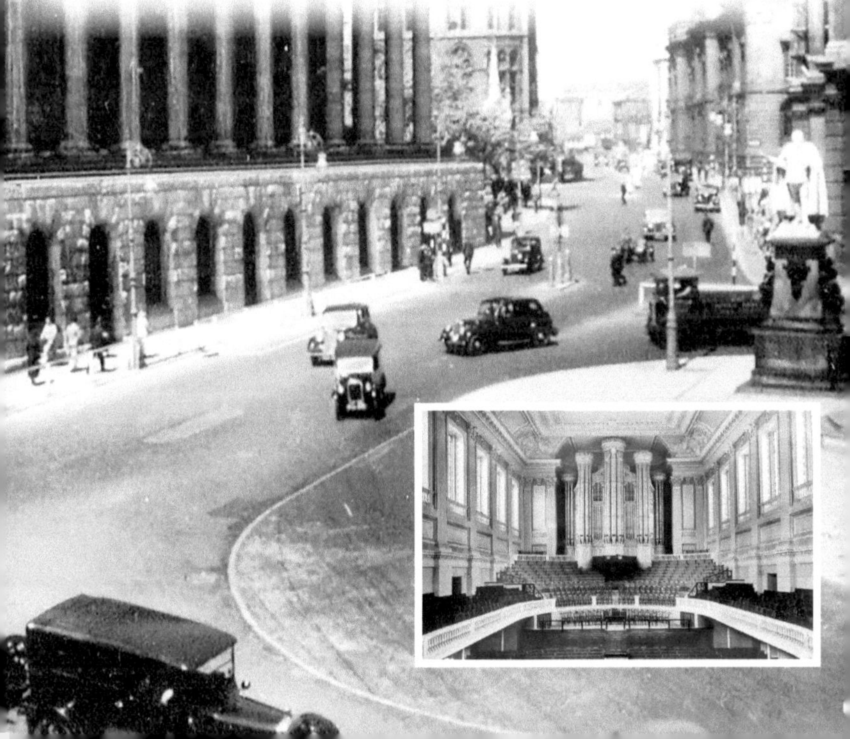

4. HEAD POST OFFICE

This third heritage building near the square's edge (built in 1891) resembles a French chateau, which was somewhat unusual in the smoky air of an industrial nineteenth-century city. For many years this building served as Birmingham's head post office. It was saved from threatened demolition by a successful public campaign for its retention.

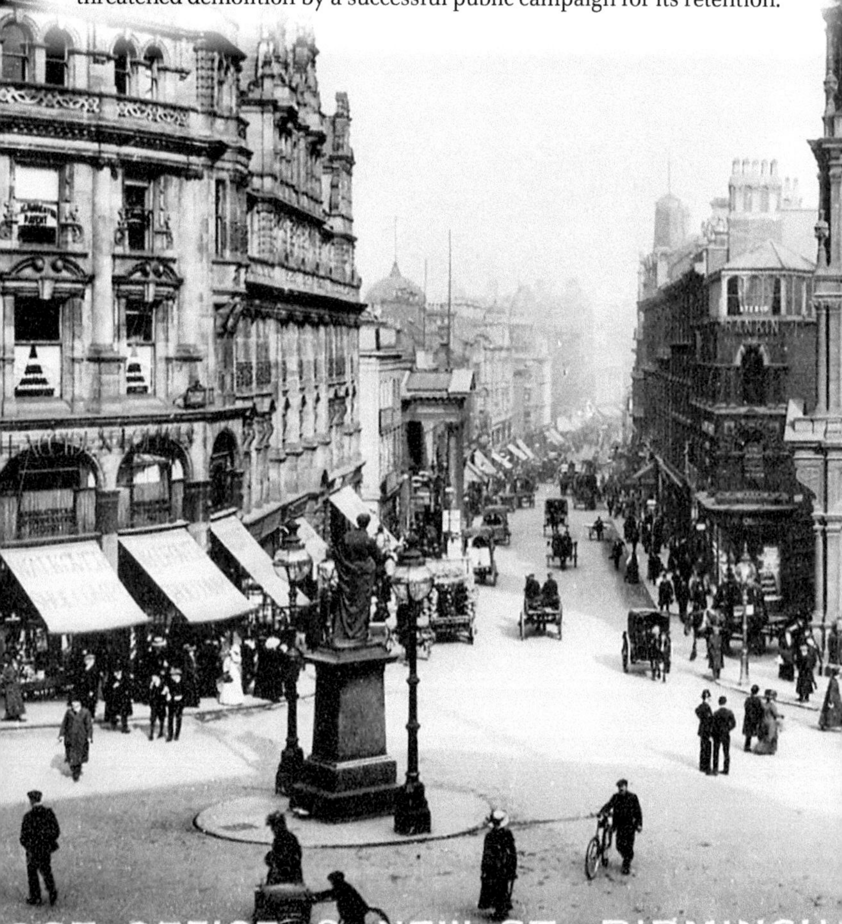

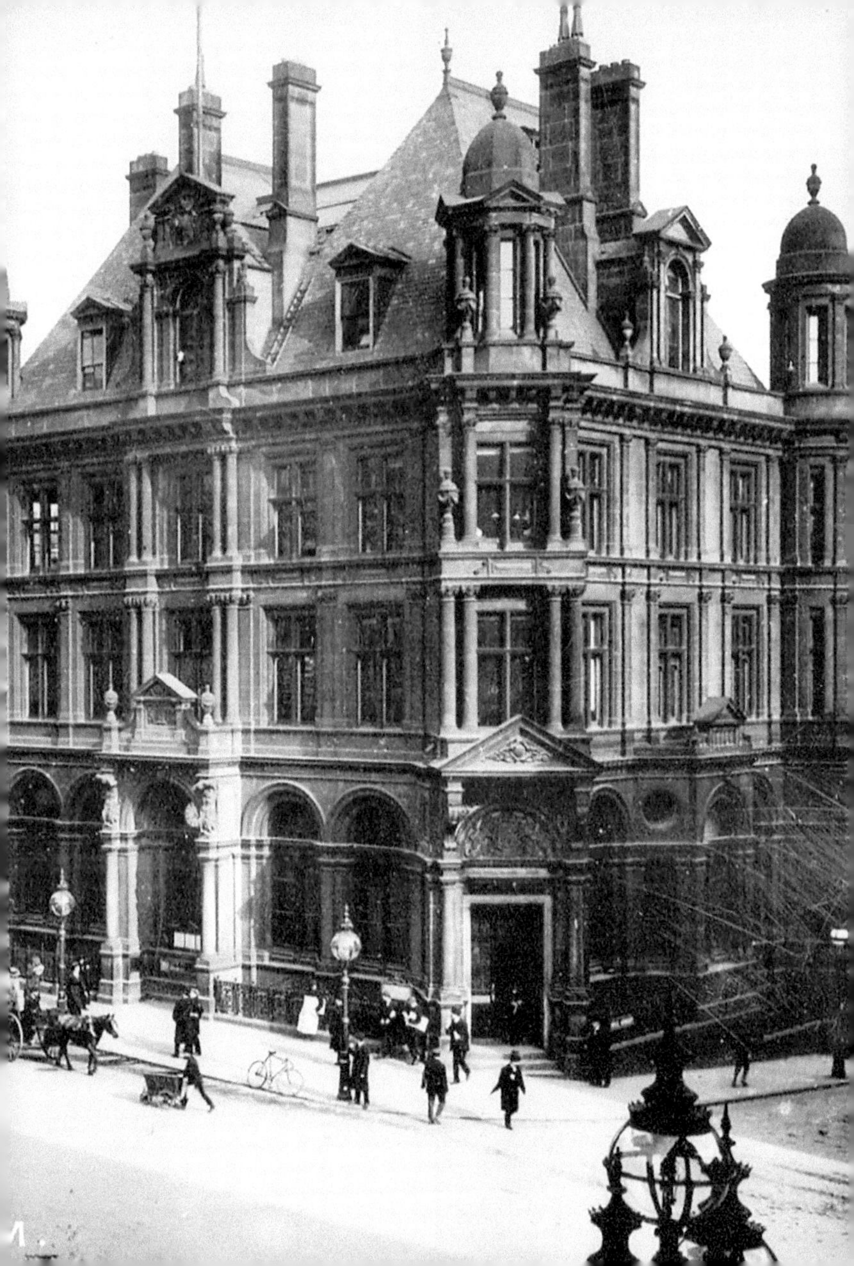
1.

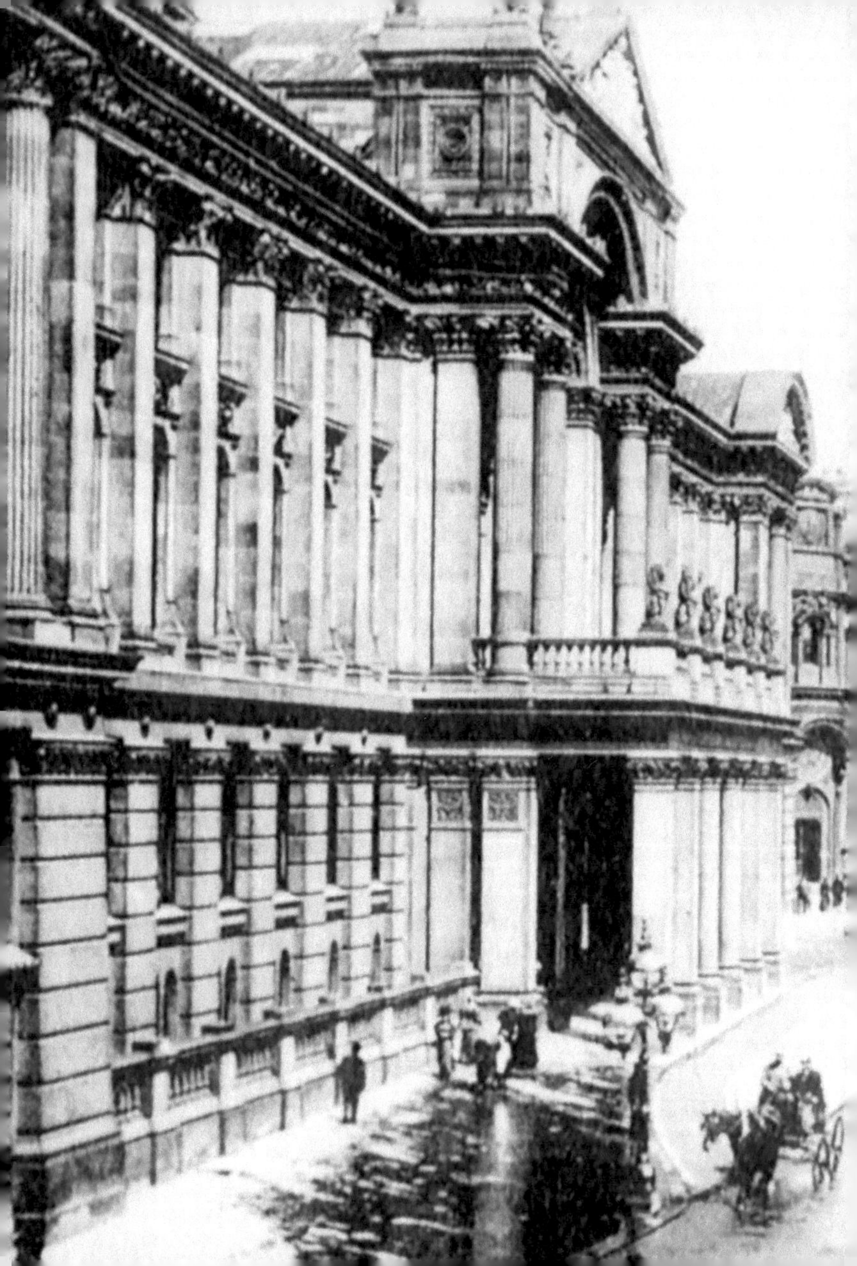

5. COUNCIL HOUSE AND COLMORE ROW

Stretching away in a north-easterly direction from the Council House, is Colmore Row. A short distance along, at No. 122–124, stands a Grade I listed building – the 1900 'office block' of Eagle Insurance. Previously, much of the row consisted of sturdy, stone buildings that were occupied by banks, and commercial enterprises.

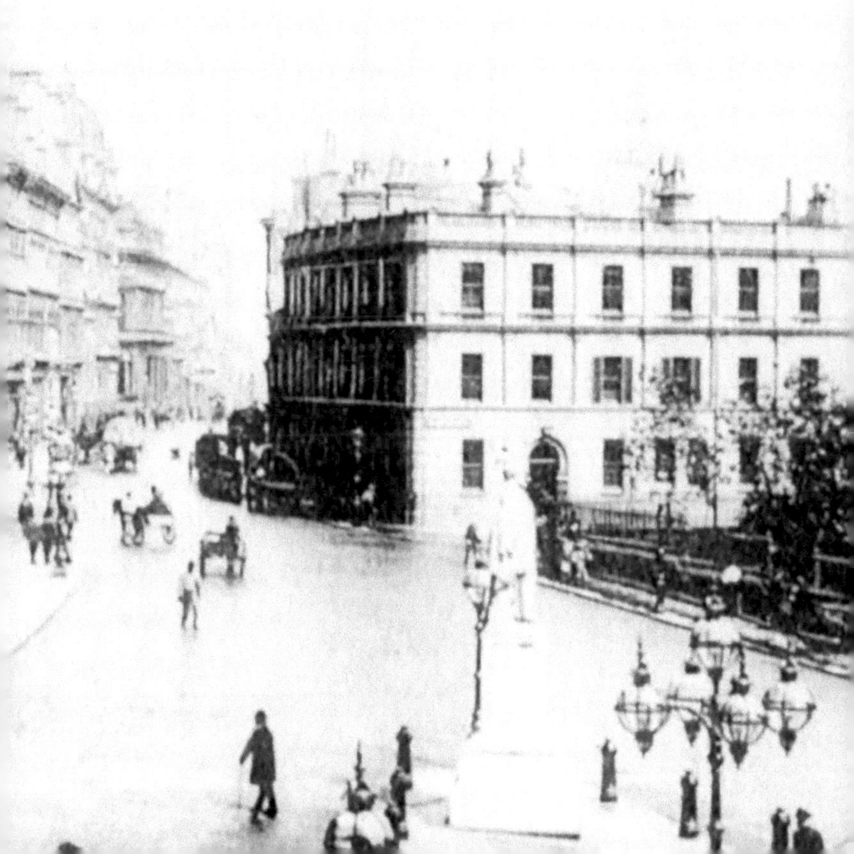

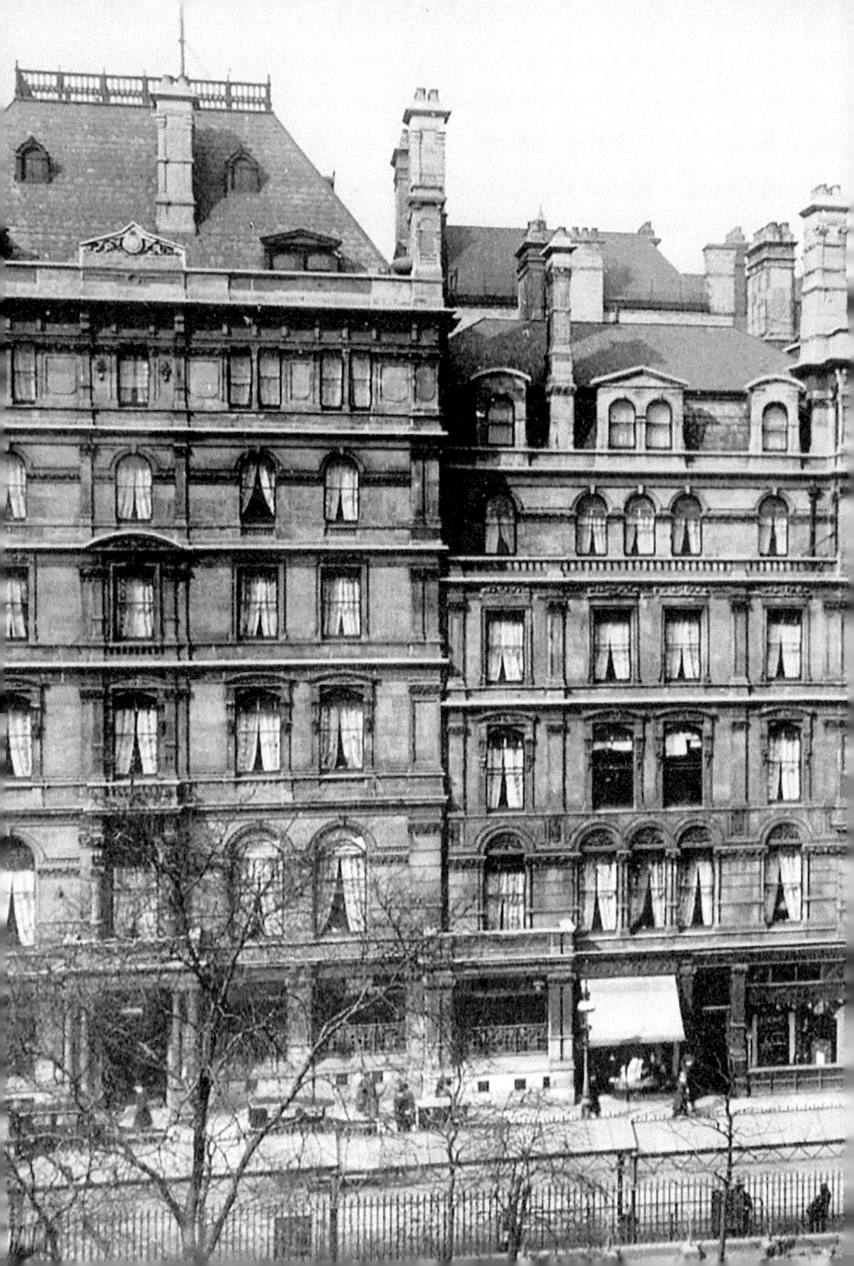

6. GRAND HOTEL

No doubt many special occasions have taken place in this Colmore Row hotel. The 'Grand', a Victorian building completed in 1880, is sited directly opposite St Philip's Cathedral and was one of the city's finest hotels.

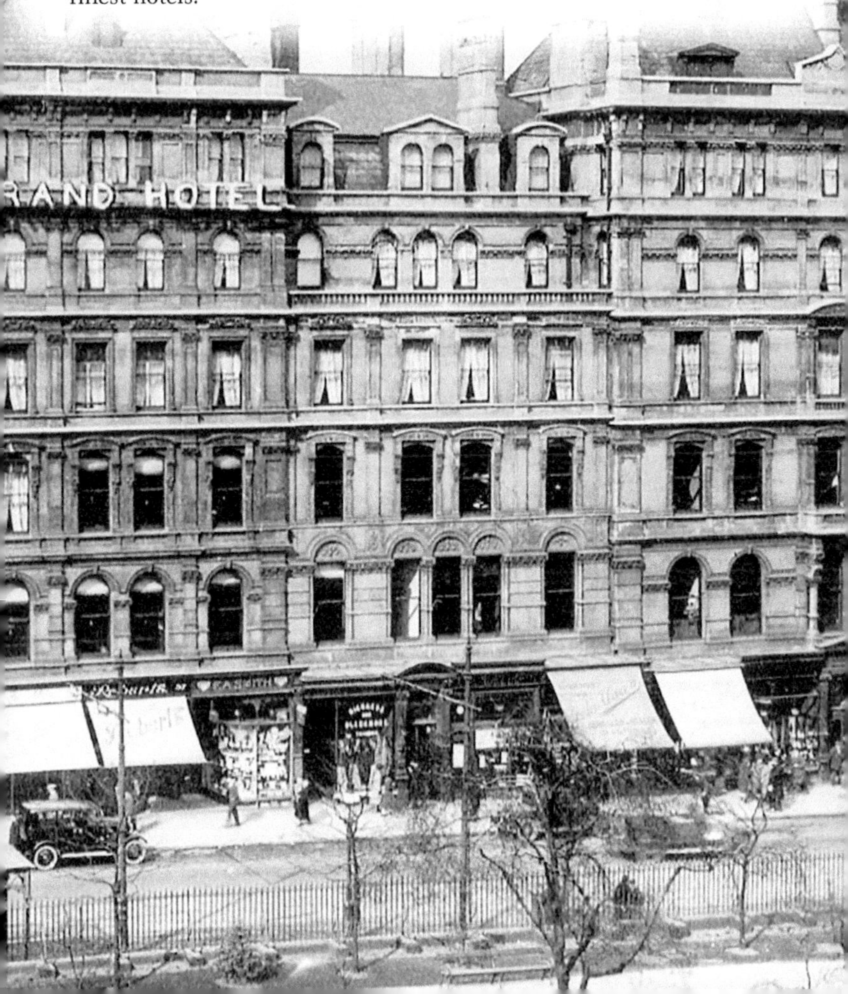

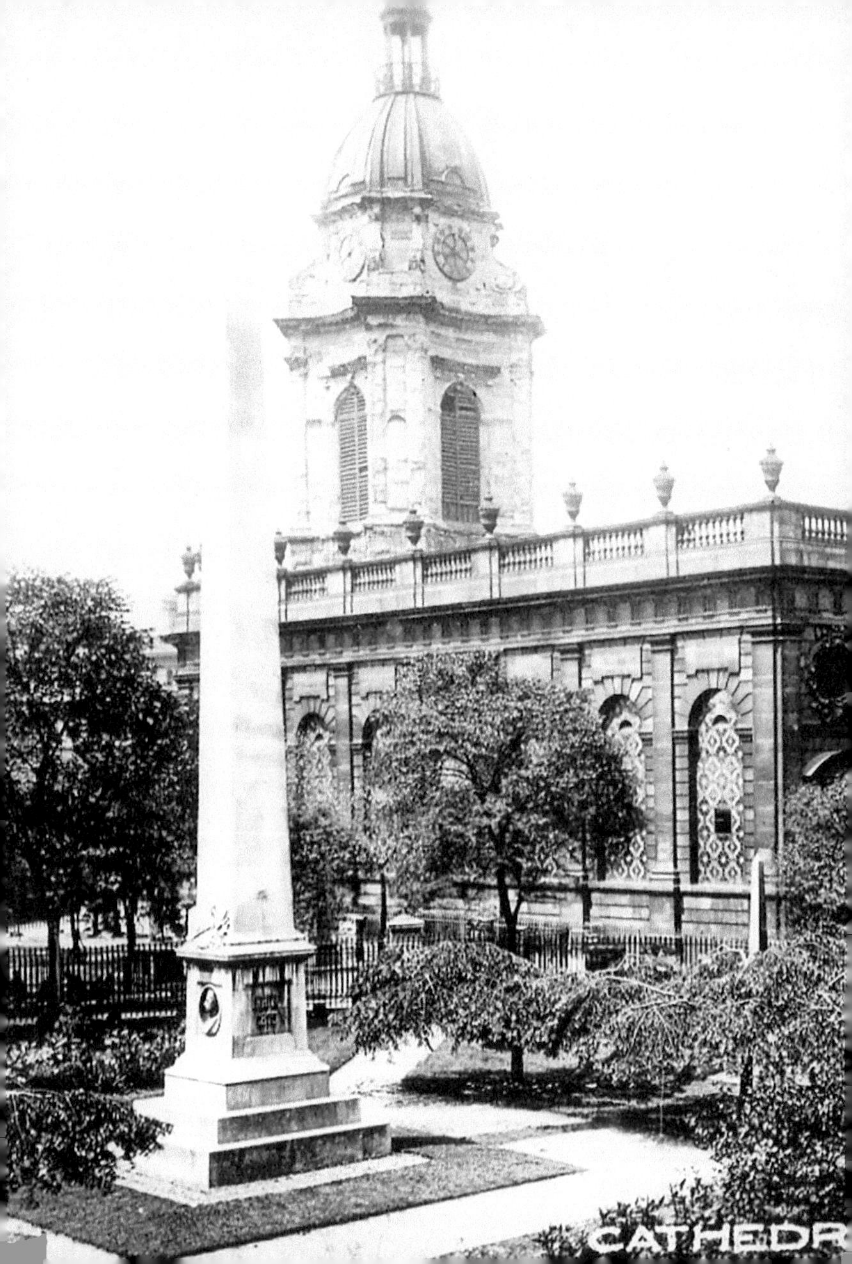
CATHEDR

7. ST PHILIP'S CATHEDRAL

Opposite the commercial buildings stood the early eighteenth-century church of St Philip's. In 1905 the church achieved cathedral status. Public paths criss-cross its grounds. 'Music in the Cathedral' concerts have been popular, and another major attraction for visitors over the years has been the stained-glass window, which was designed by local artist Burne-Jones. This postcard is franked 1915.

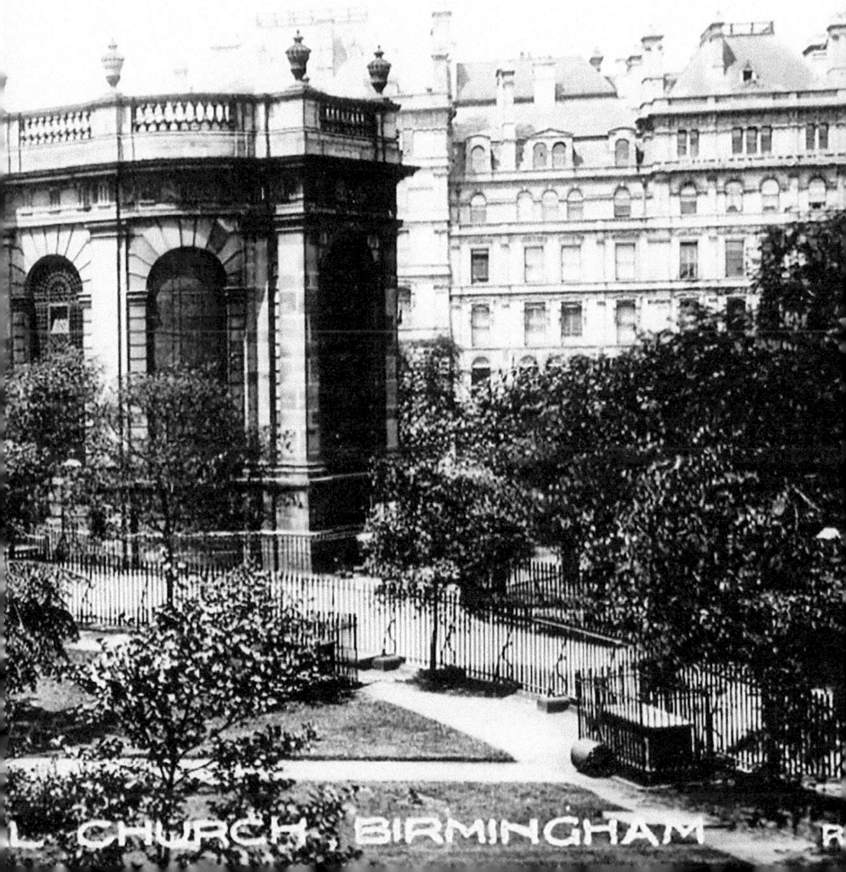

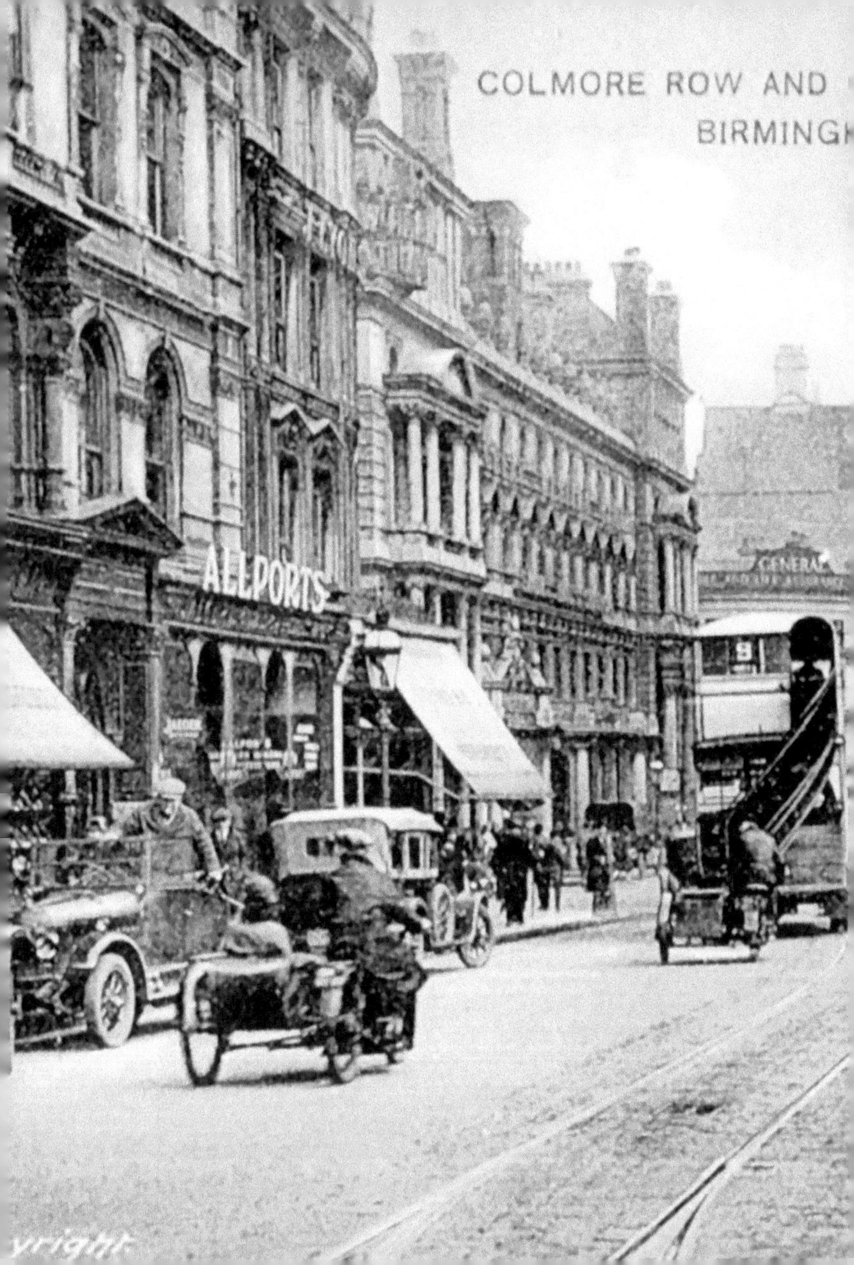

COLMORE ROW AND
BIRMINGH
ALLPORTS
GENERAL

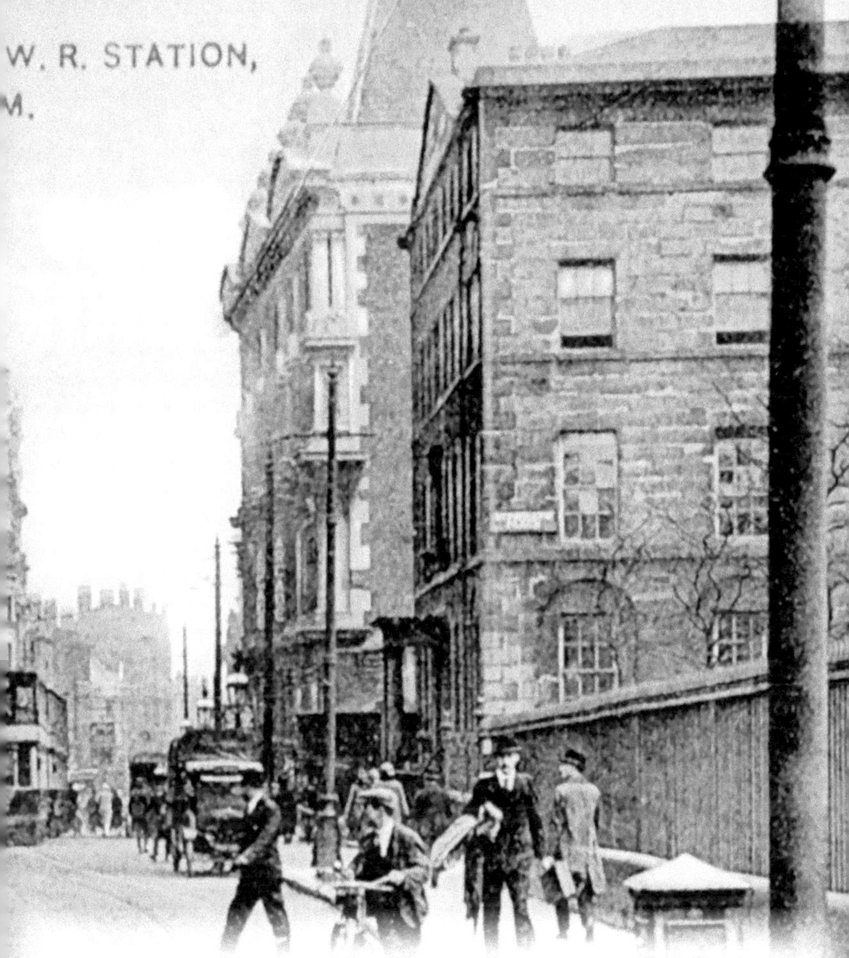

8. COLMORE ROW

This image shows the bustling activity between the two world wars, visible is a tram at its terminus close to the entrance of Snow Hill Railway Station, a bus with an open-air staircase to the top deck, and a motorbike with a sidecar.

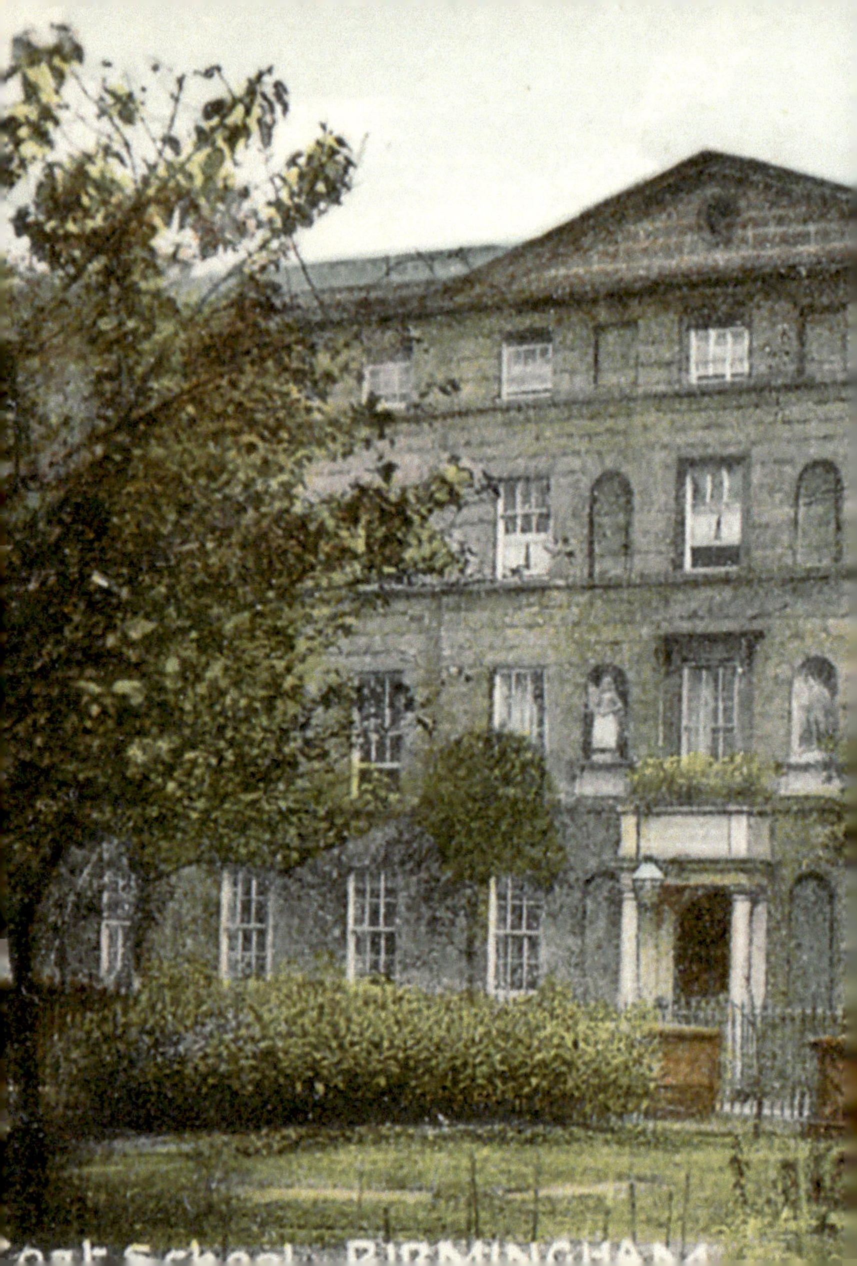
School, BIRMINGHAM

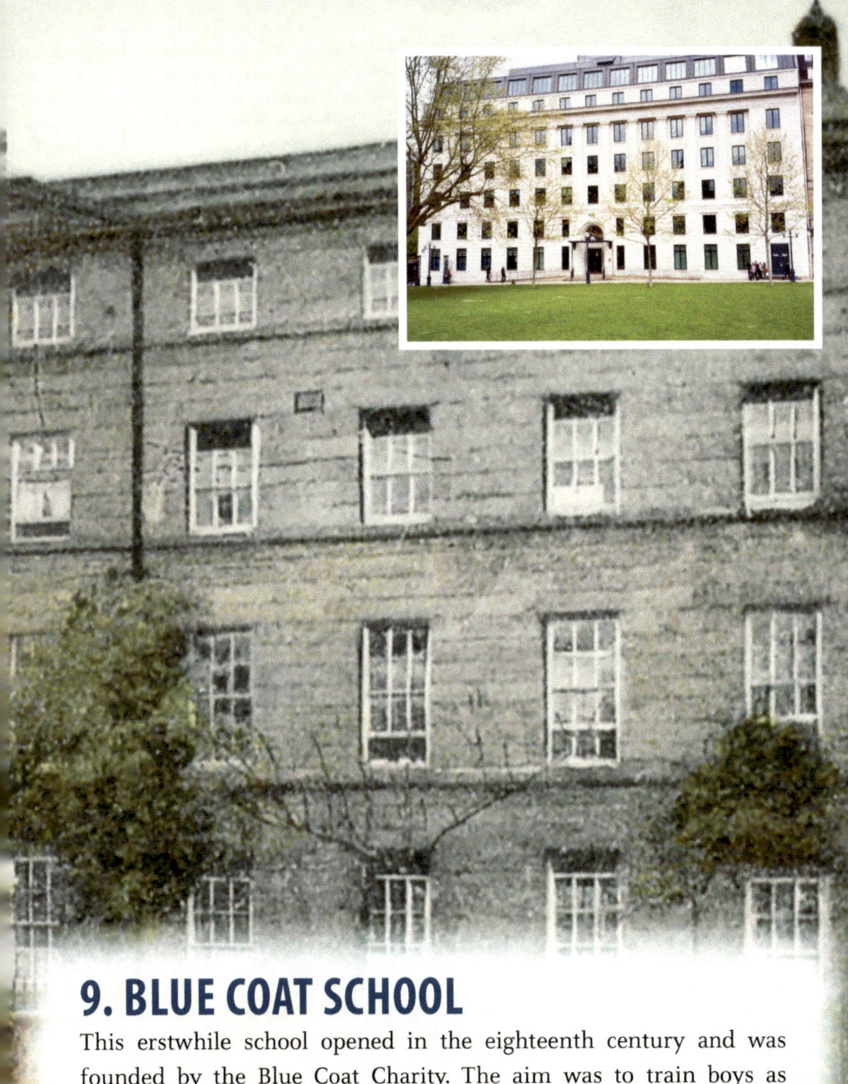

9. BLUE COAT SCHOOL

This erstwhile school opened in the eighteenth century and was founded by the Blue Coat Charity. The aim was to train boys as apprentices and girls as domestic servants. The school left the building in 1930, moving to the leafy Birmingham suburb of Harborne.

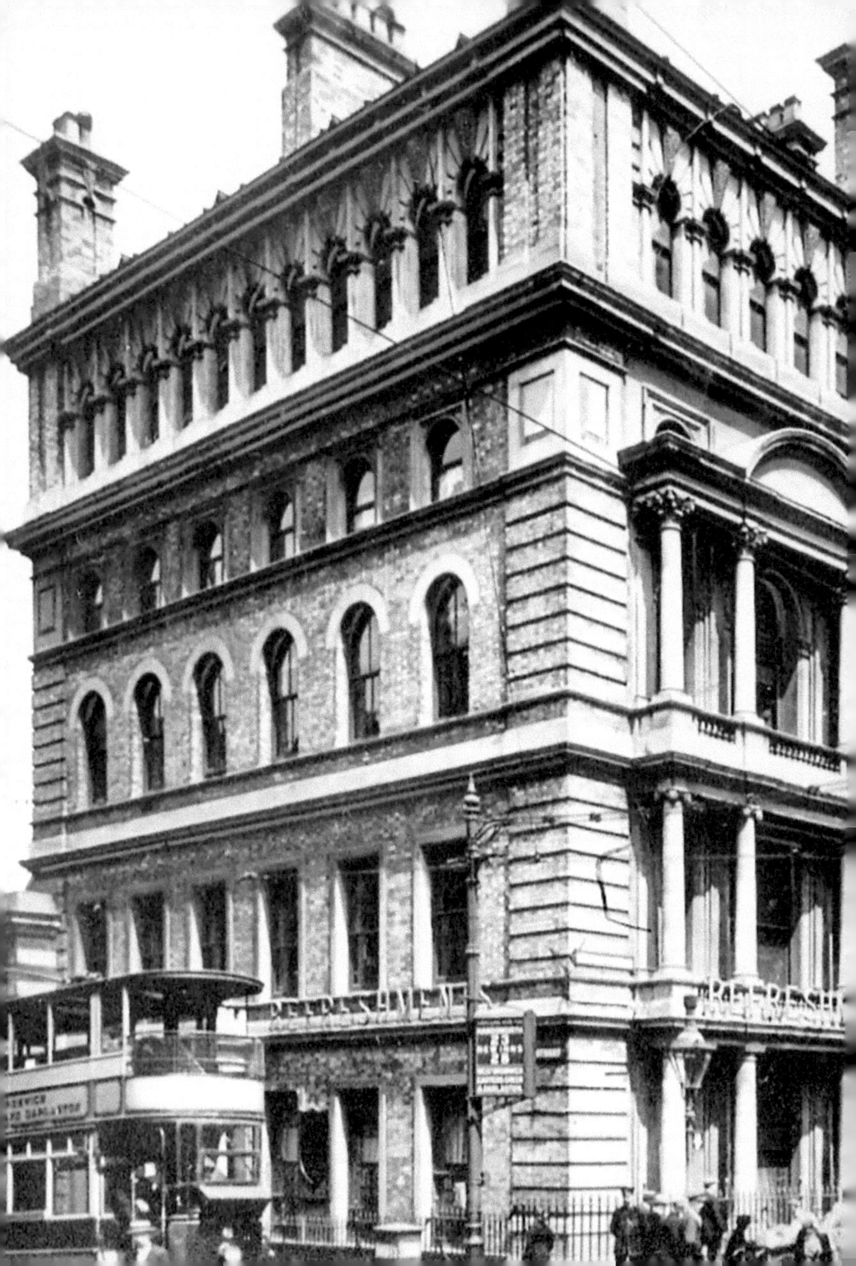
REFRESH

10. SNOW HILL STATION

An imposing railway hotel, typical of its day, after opening in 1863, Snow Hill Station (entry via Colmore Row) became a major player in the extensive network of the Great Western Railway. Sometime after the Second World War, the station went through a bad period; it was later reborn in a modern form but had much fewer services. The tram shown on the postcard has reached the top of Livery Street.

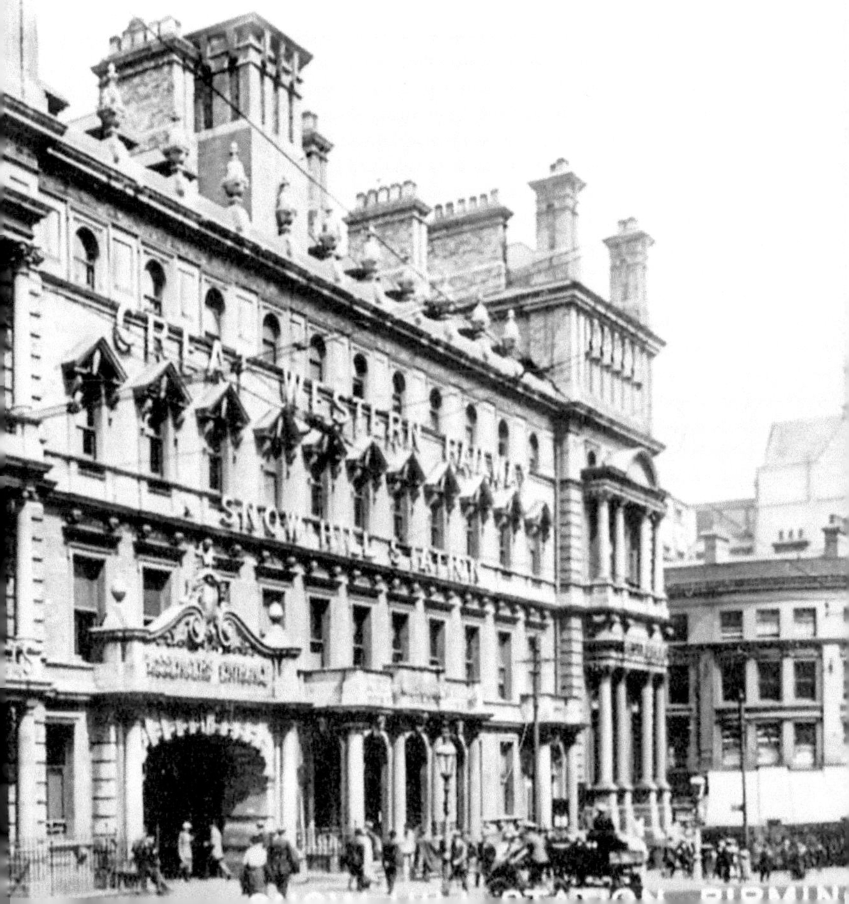

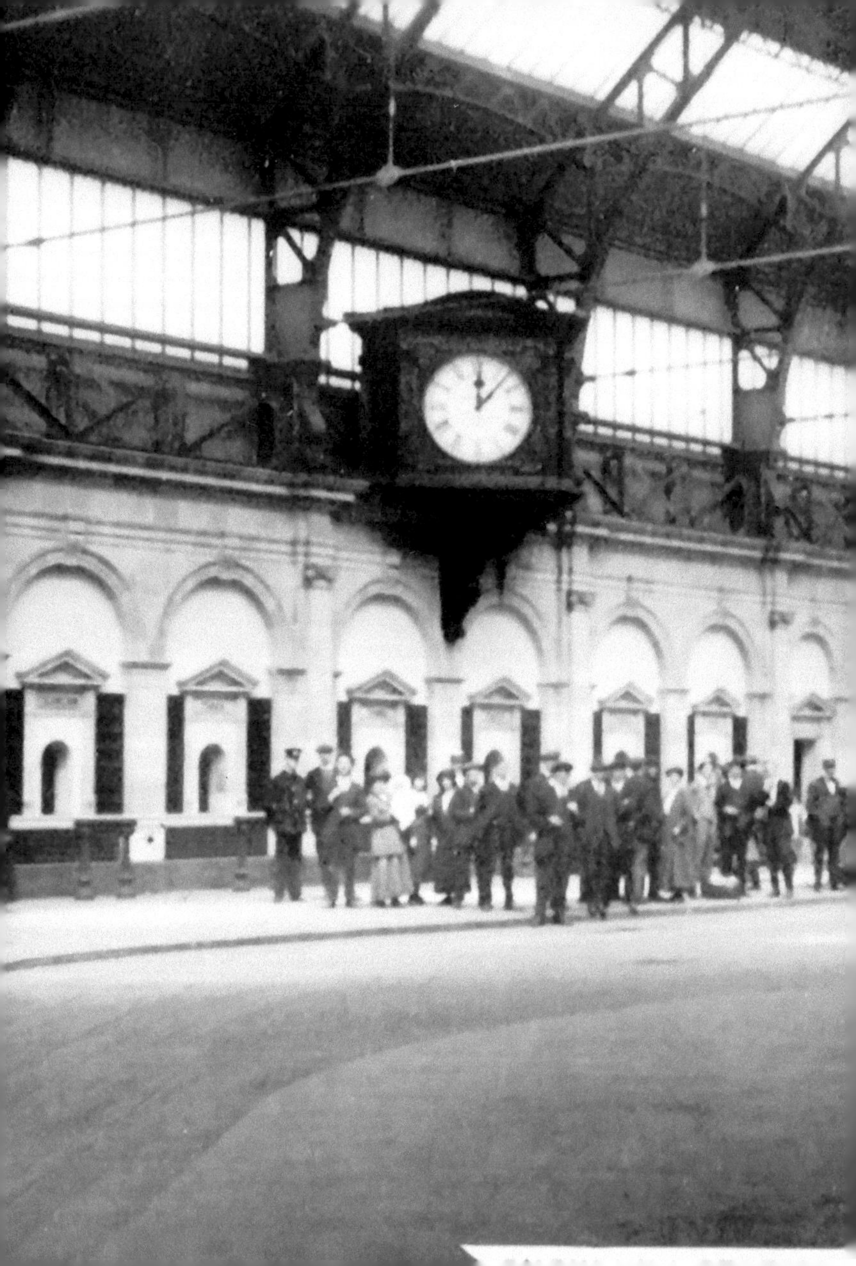

11. SNOW HILL STATION BOOKING OFFICE

A short tunnel through the hotel gave access to a spacious, stately, light and airy booking office, featuring a row of dignified, handsome ticket stands. The massive clock became something of a landmark and a meeting place for locals, 'Meet me here on Saturday at 3 in the afternoon and we'll go to the new milk bar.' It is useful to remember that during the interwar years, the normal working week was five and a half days, and for many transport to the city meant bus or tram journeys.

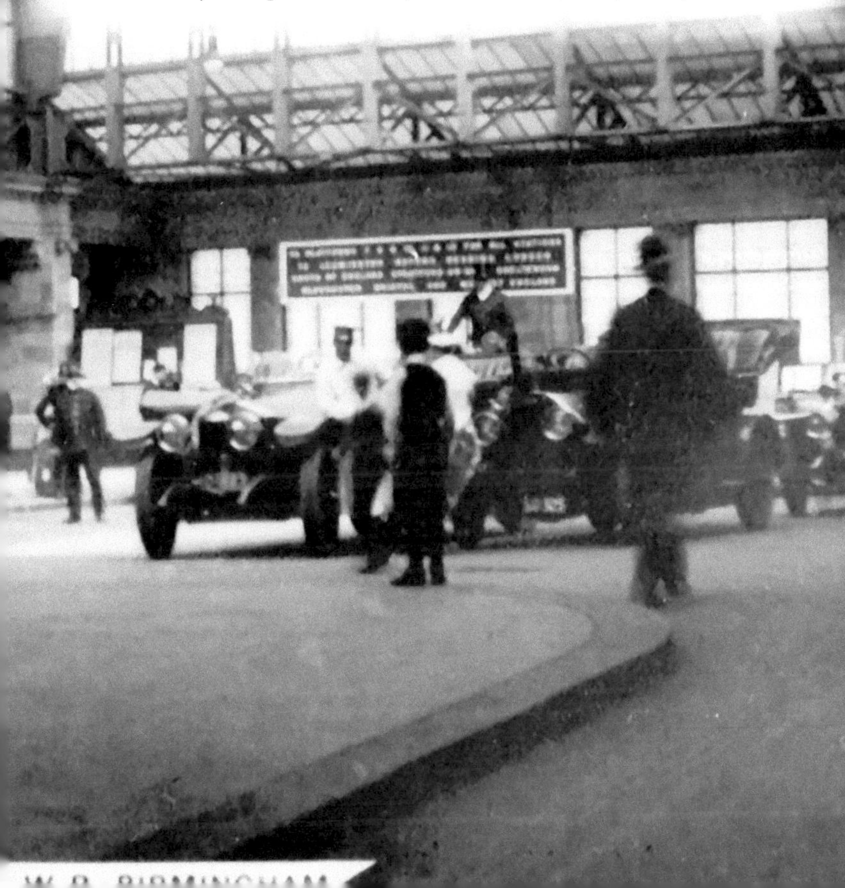

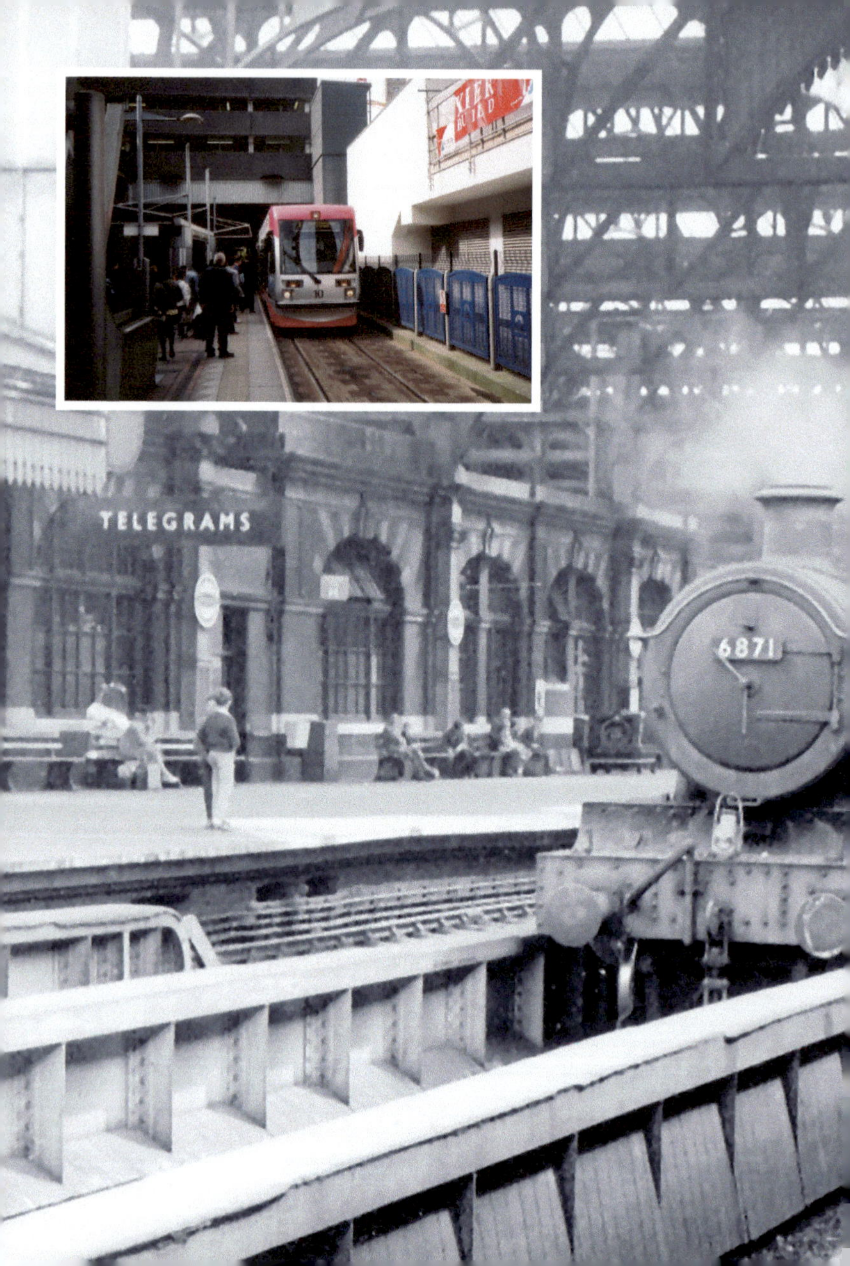
TELEGRAMS
6871

12. SNOW HILL STATION PLATFORMS

The steam-driven railway engine can evoke a myriad of memories – troop trains during two world wars, the evacuation of school children during 1939, and so on. In peacetime, Snow Hill Station became popular with many local Birmingham folk as it was the starting place for increasing numbers of holidaymakers heading south-west to Paignton and Torquay, or north-west to Rhyl and Colwyn Bay in Wales.

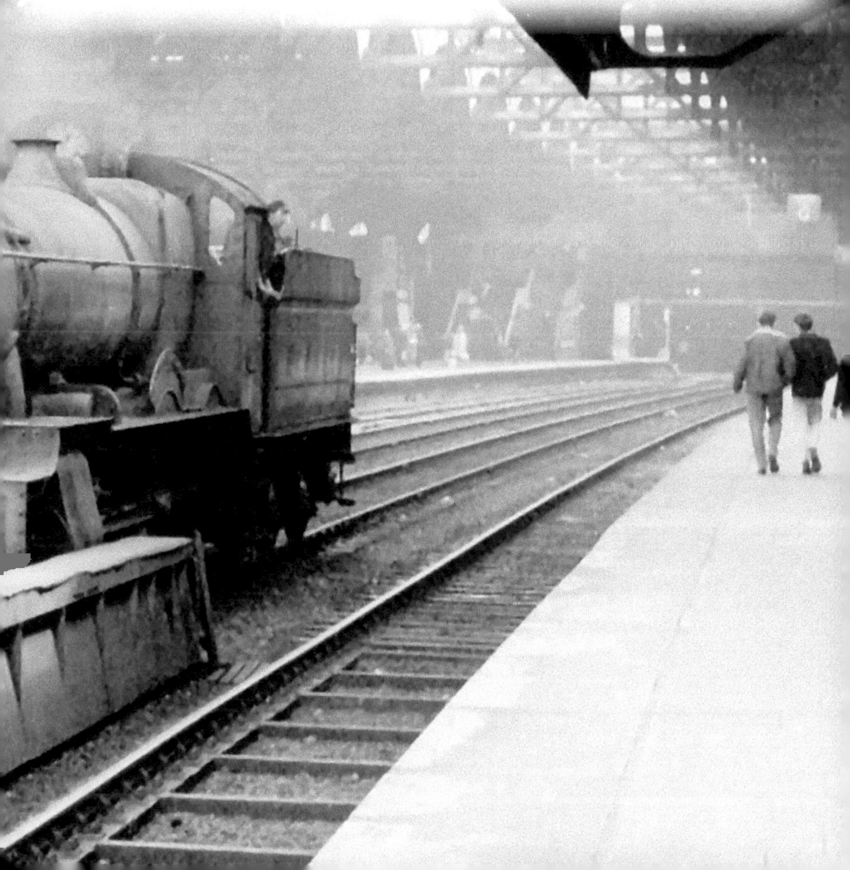

13. GREAT WESTERN ARCADE, COLMORE ROW

Between the tramlines runs a narrow duct, along which a steel cable moves continuously. The car could be attached to or released from the cable as the driver determined. The cable-car system shown was introduced in 1888 and ran from Colmore Row to Hockley Brook – no shelter from the weather on top deck!

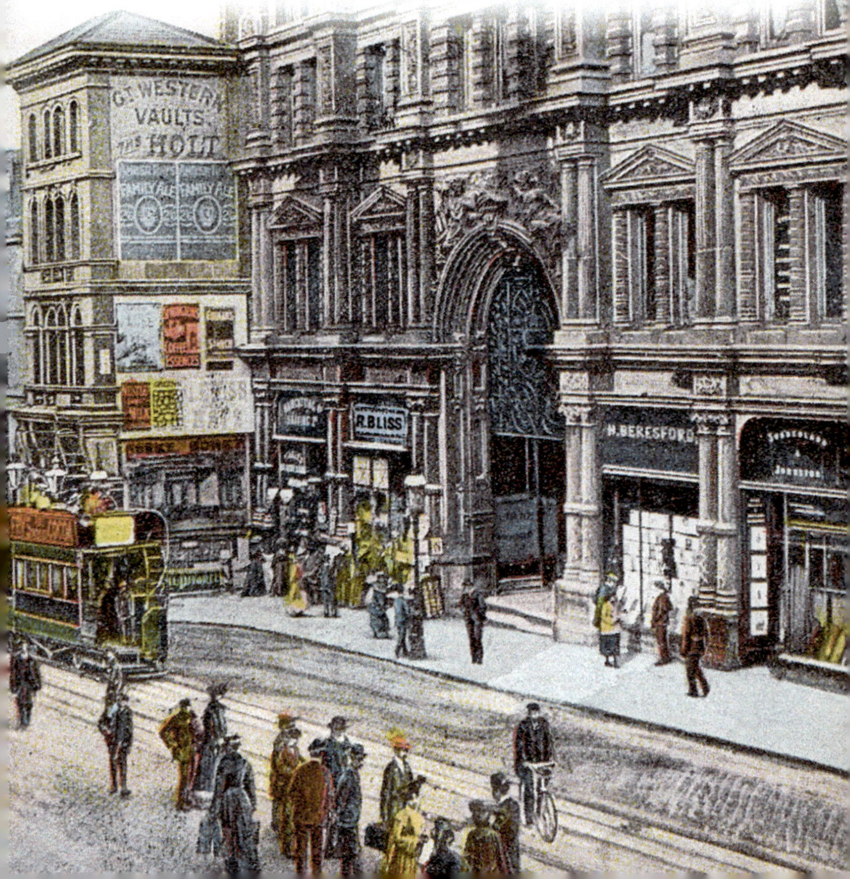

14. GREAT WESTERN ARCADE, INTERIOR

Built in 1875–76 directly above a railway tunnel, this elegant arcade (looking towards Temple Row) was free of traffic, offering shelter from the elements and an array of quality goods, appealing to shoppers with enticing arrangements.

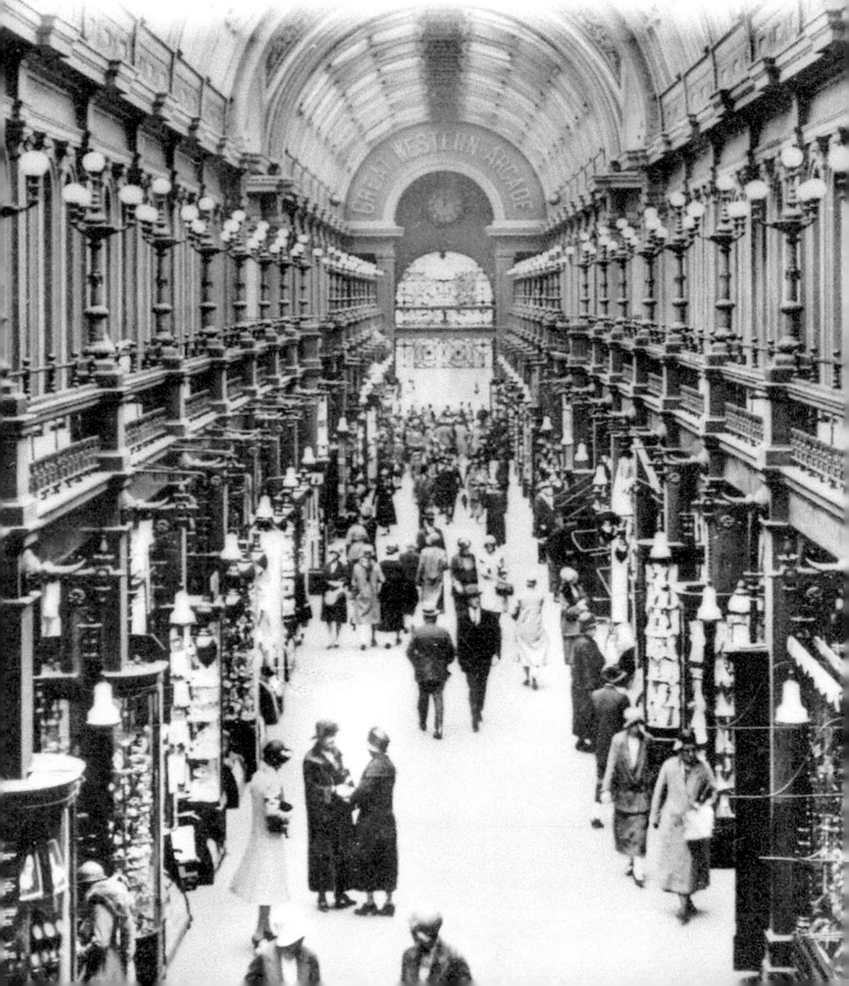

15. COLMORE ROW, SNOW HILL

This image shows a view from the end of Colmore Row of the impressive Snow Hill railway station and hotel. To the right, Snow Hill drops away and part of the platform area of the station can be seen. Even the corner buffet transmits an air of dignity and confidence.

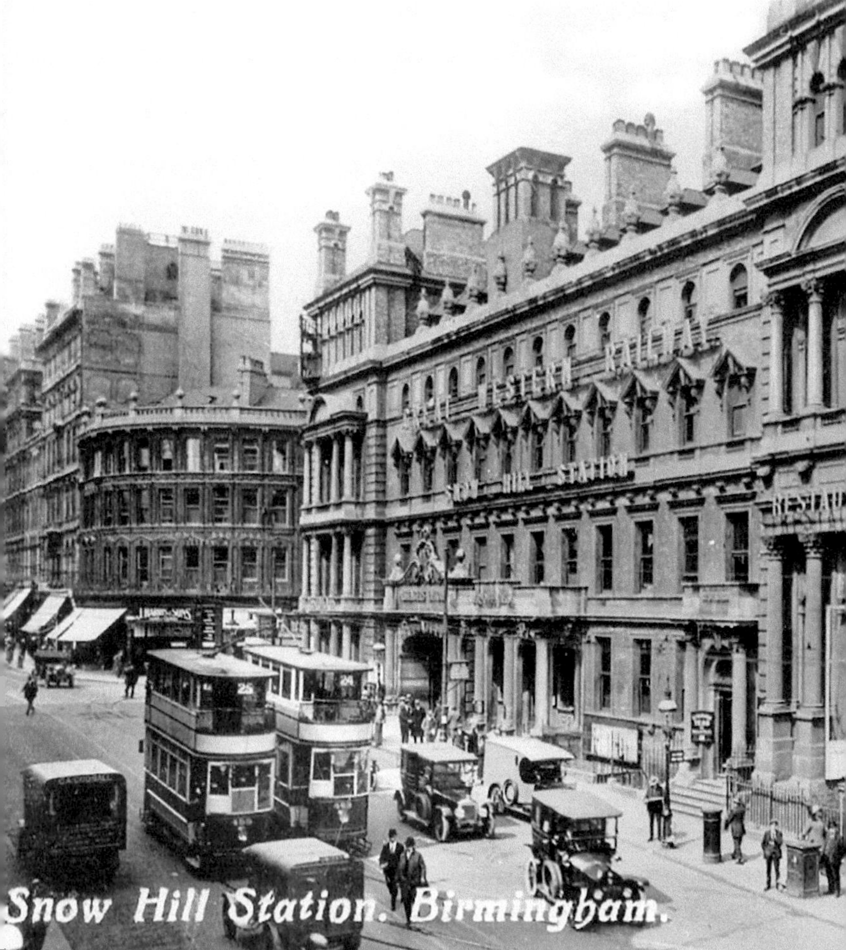

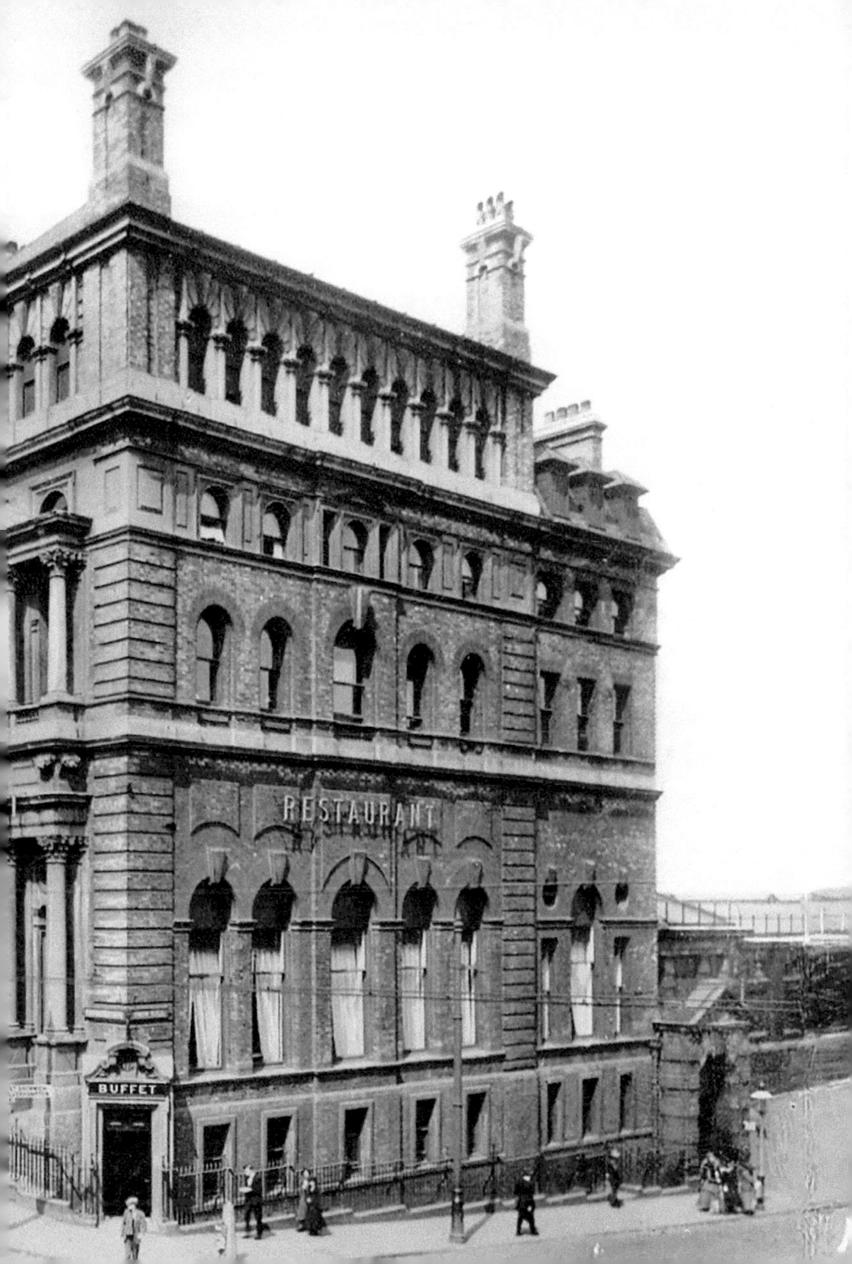

RESTAURANT
BUFFET

16. STEELHOUSE LANE

Steelhouse Lane was so named because of its earlier life of metal working. The card shows, in a new form, how some steel has reached its city centre terminus. The last Birmingham electric tram ran in 1953. Built during the 'golden age' of movies, the Gaumont opened in 1931 and became one of Birmingham's most popular cinemas.

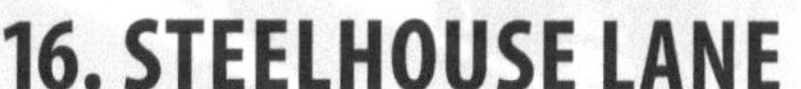

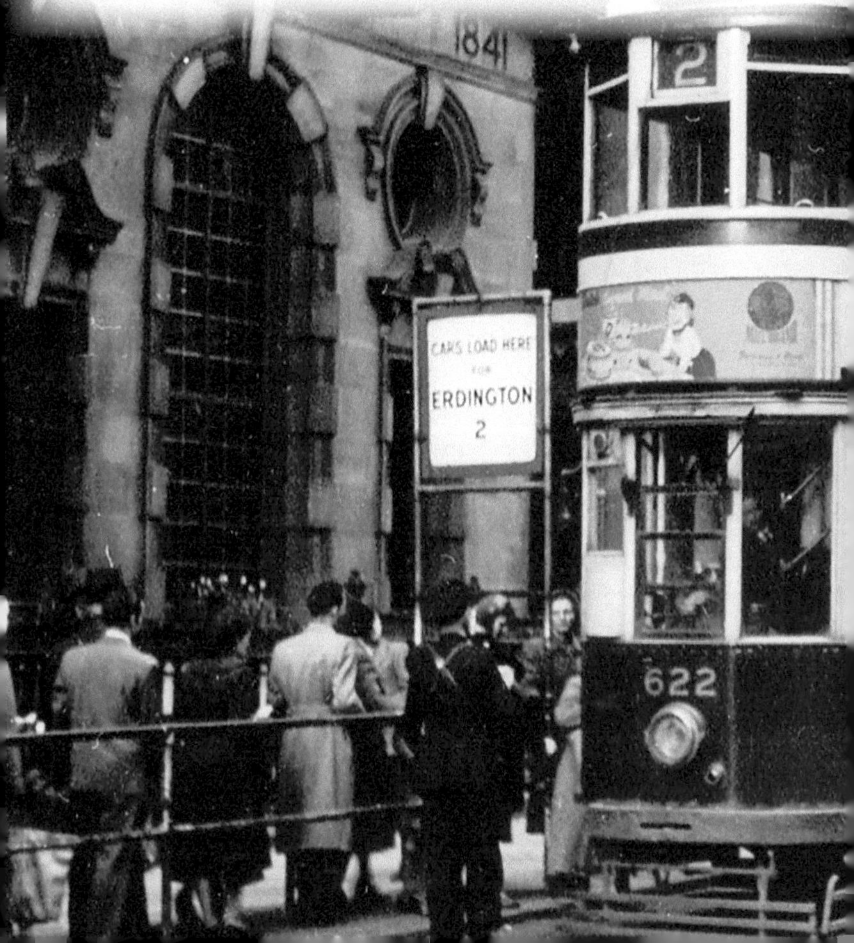

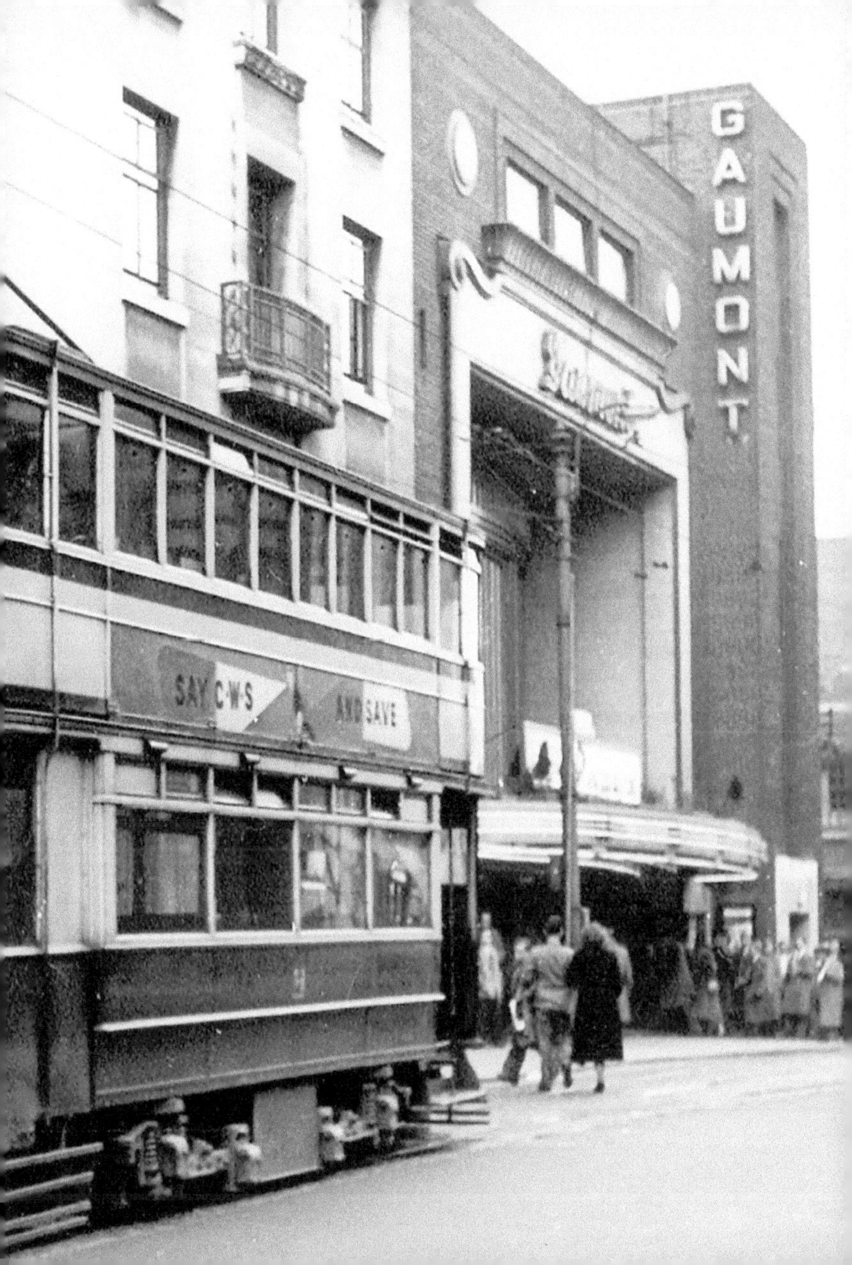

GAUMONT
SAY CWS AND SAVE

17. GENERAL HOSPITAL, STEELHOUSE LANE

This Victorian red-brick hospital opened in 1897, replacing an eighteenth-century one. Known as 'the General', it had 340 beds. It remained the city's leading hospital until the 1930s.

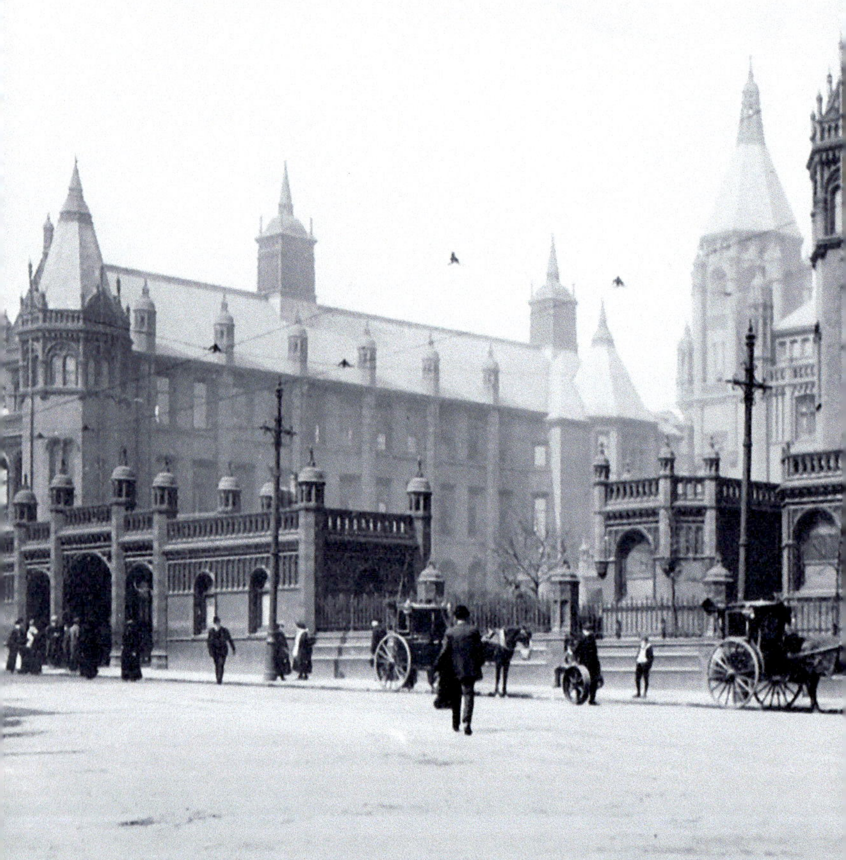

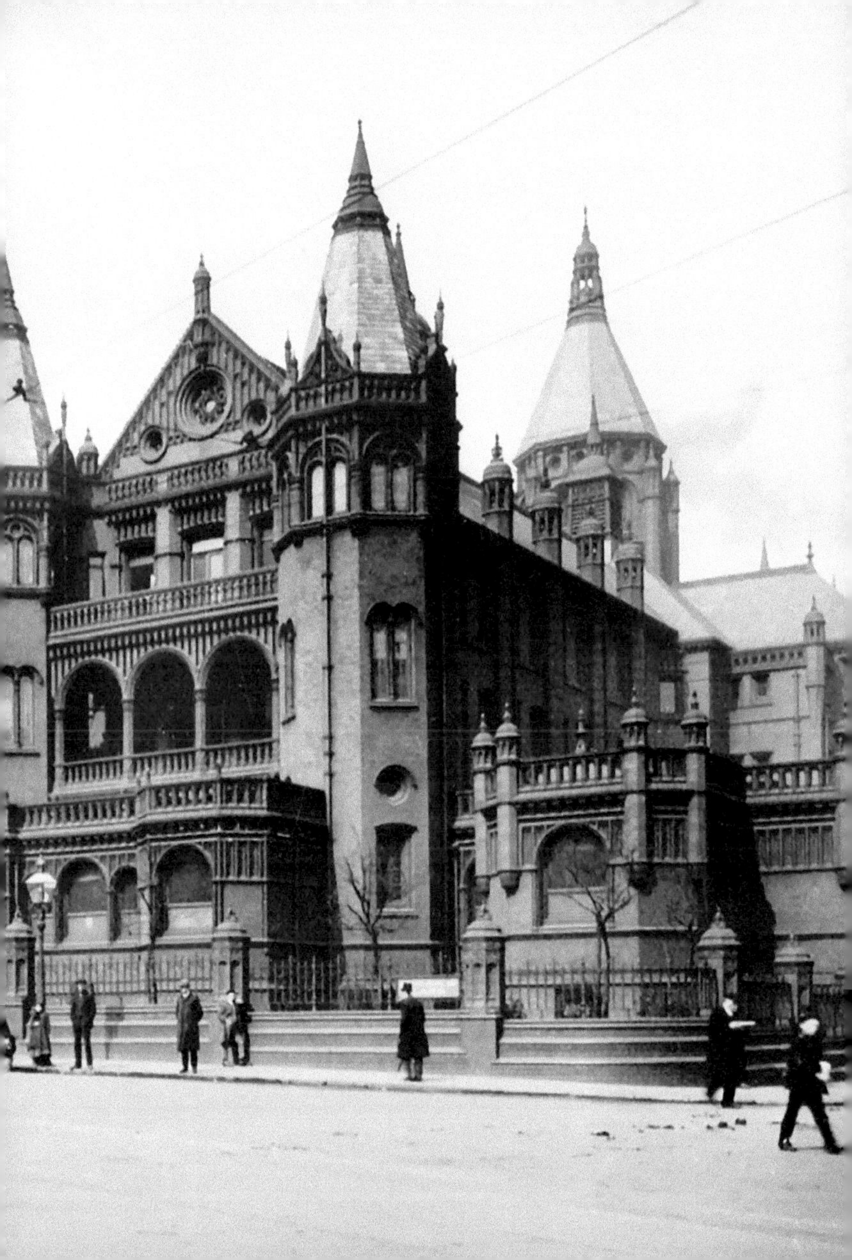

18. CENTRAL FIRE STATION, LANCASTER SQUARE

Of typical 1930s style and designed for a very specific purpose, this uncluttered station was triangular in shape with an interior yard. A row of garage bays for the fire engines can be seen in this image, along with a tunnel-like entrance in the tower. The fire brigade's mettle was severely tested in the air raids of 1940–41 and not found wanting.

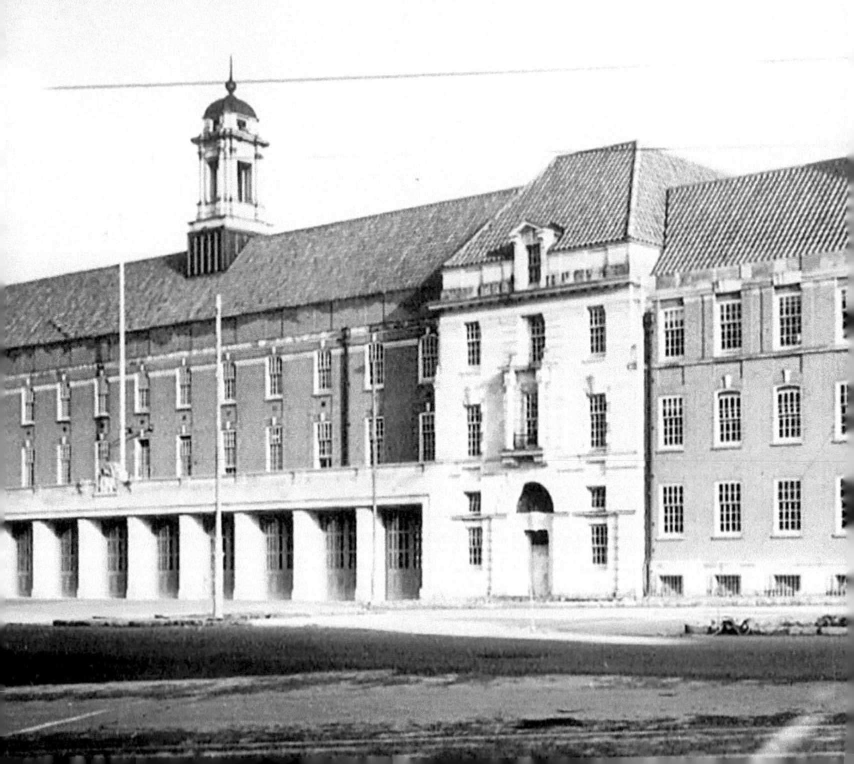

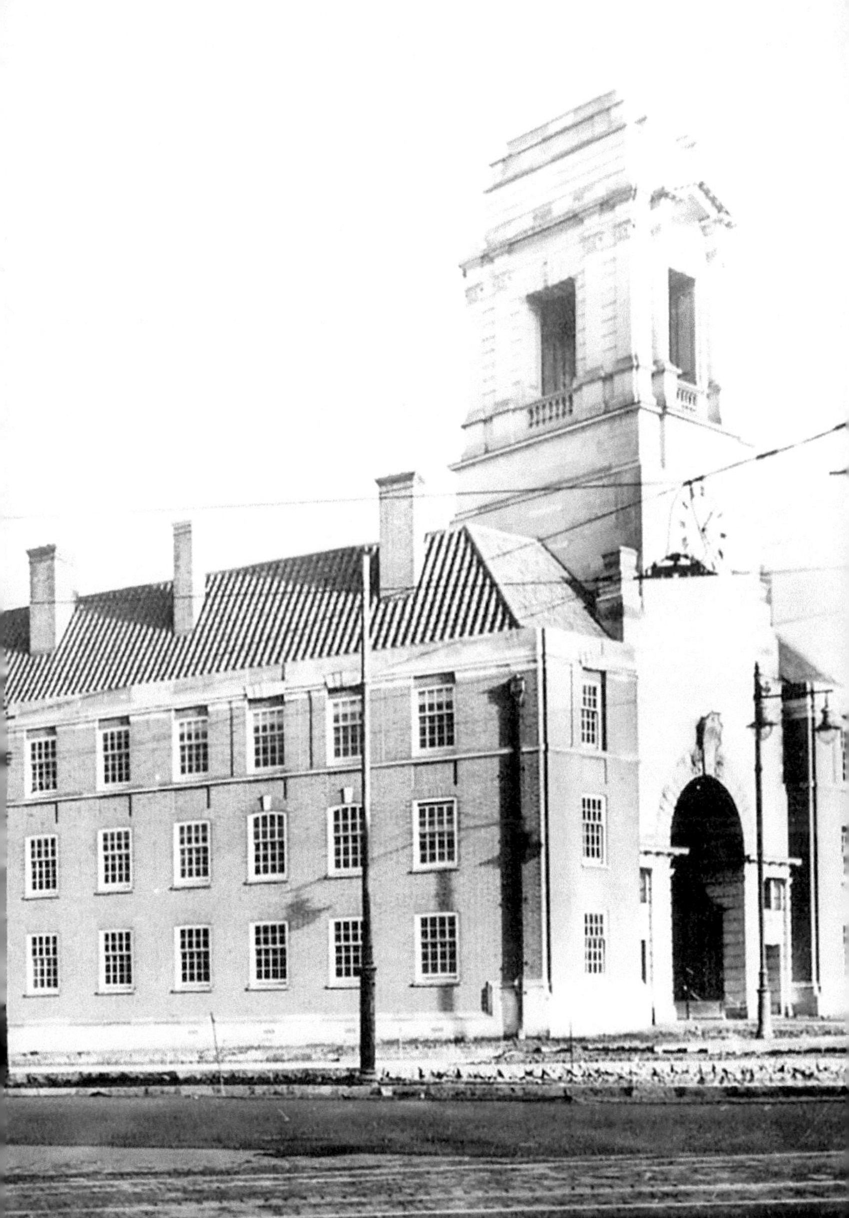

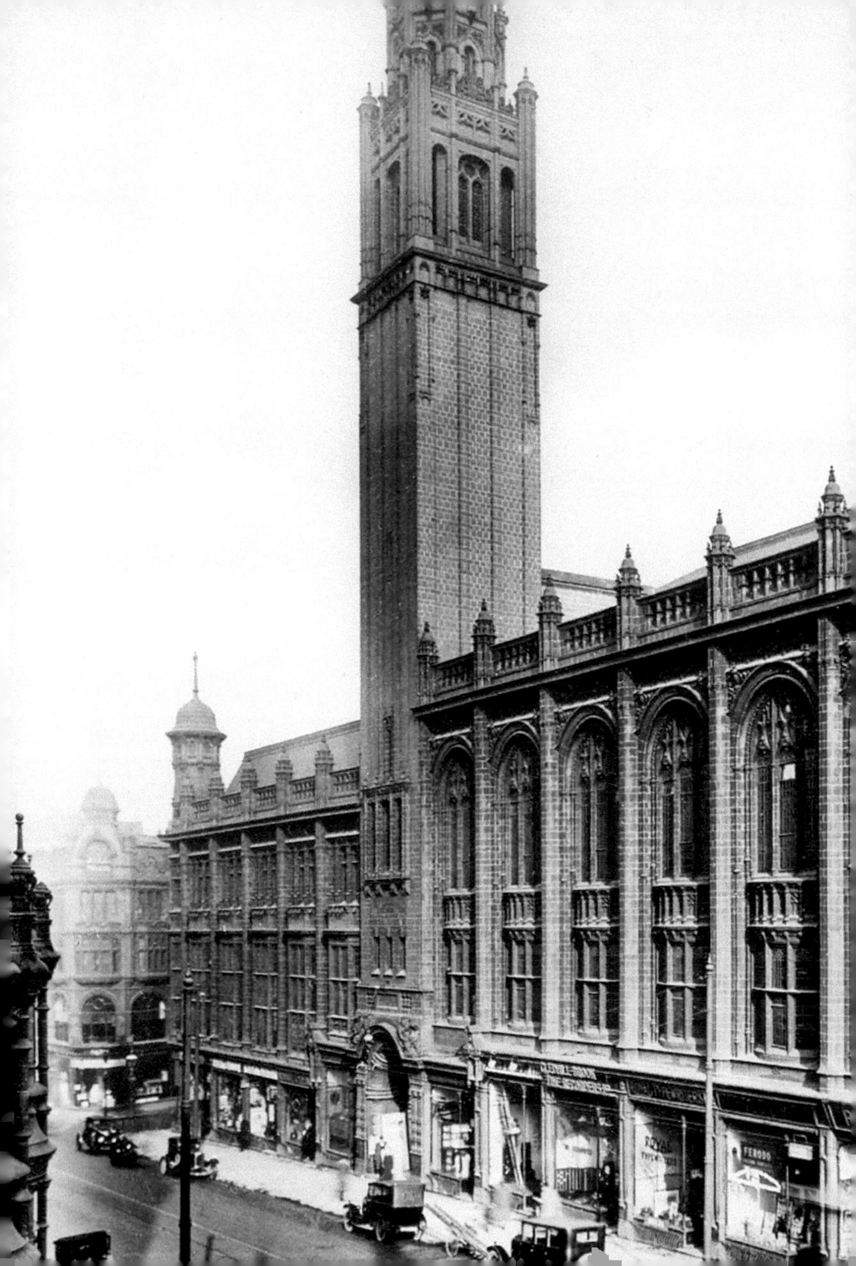

19. CORPORATION STREET AND CENTRAL HALL

Another fine red-brick building to endure the sooty air of 'the workshop of the world'. It was built in 1903 as the headquarters for local Methodists. The architecture of the hall has received high praise from distinguished expert on architectural matters, Sir Nikolaus Pevsner.

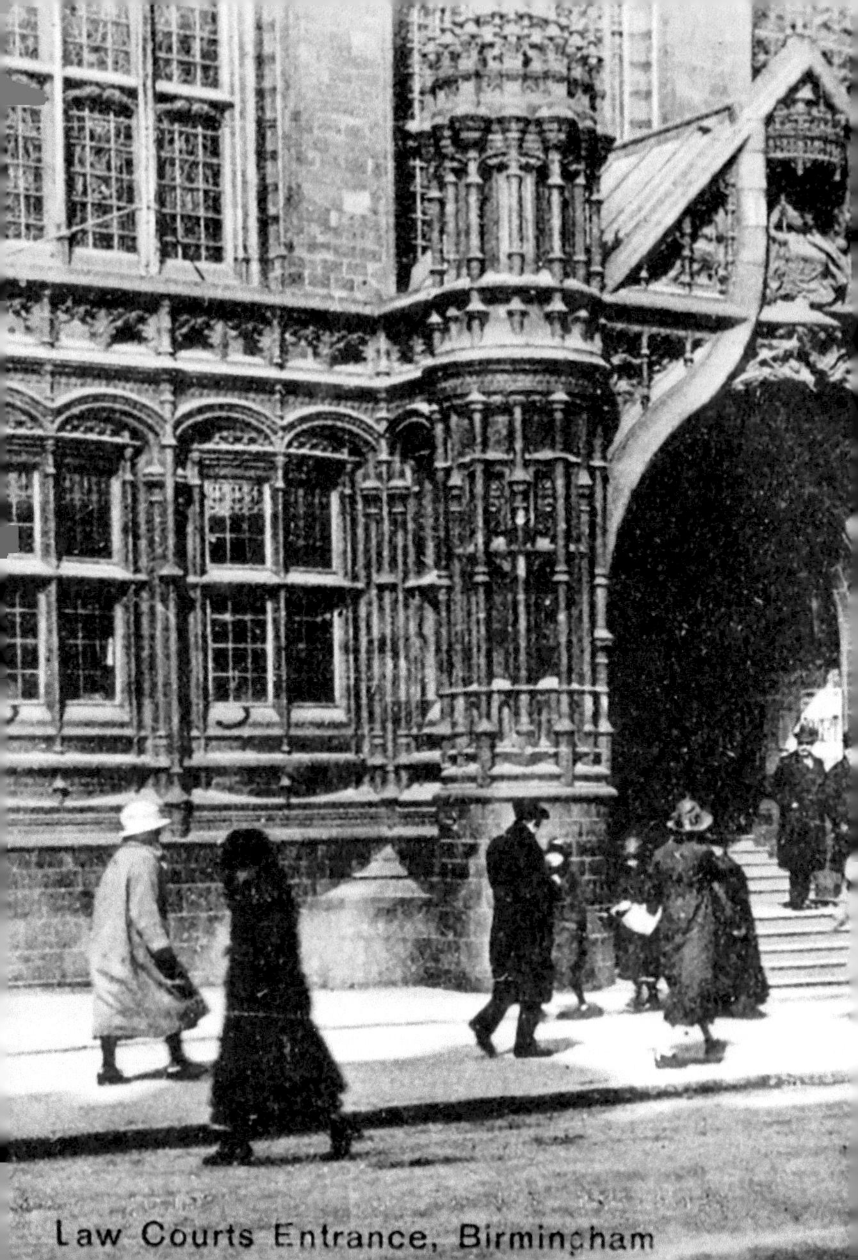

Law Courts Entrance, Birmingham

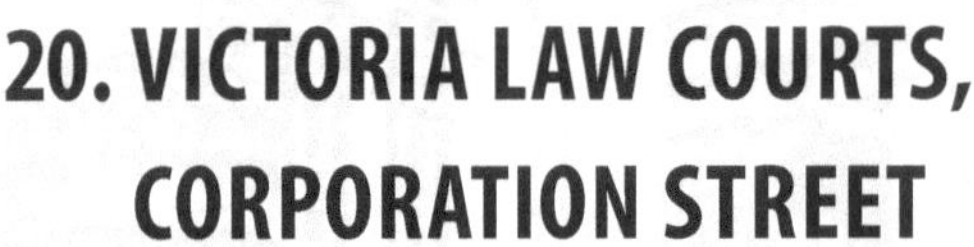

20. VICTORIA LAW COURTS, CORPORATION STREET

Almost directly across the road from Central Hall stands another fine red-brick building, the suitably magisterial in appearance, Law Courts (currently Grade I listed). It was built in 1887–91 and Queen Victoria herself laid the foundation stone.

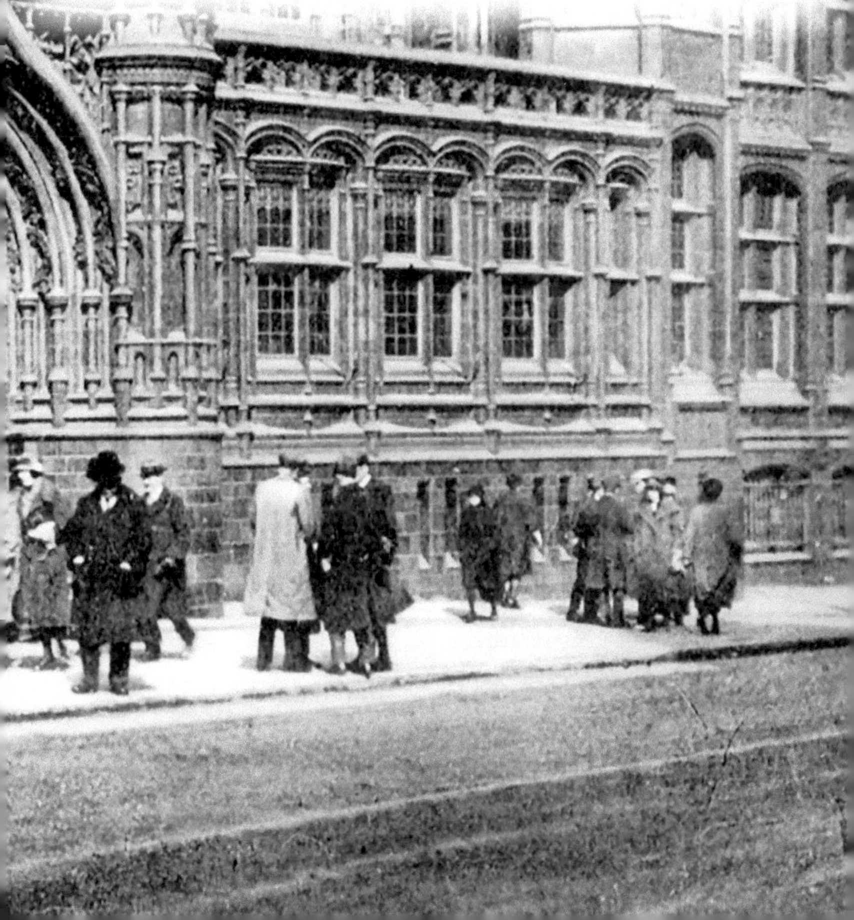

21. OLD SQUARE, CORPORATION STREET

The steam tram (at the bottom right) throws light on the age of this photograph. Steam trams in Birmingham were introduced in 1884, and ceased to operate in 1907. The railed-off area (bottom left) shields the below-ground public conveniences. These early public toilets required women to pay a fee of 1*d*, hence origin of the term 'going to spend a penny'.

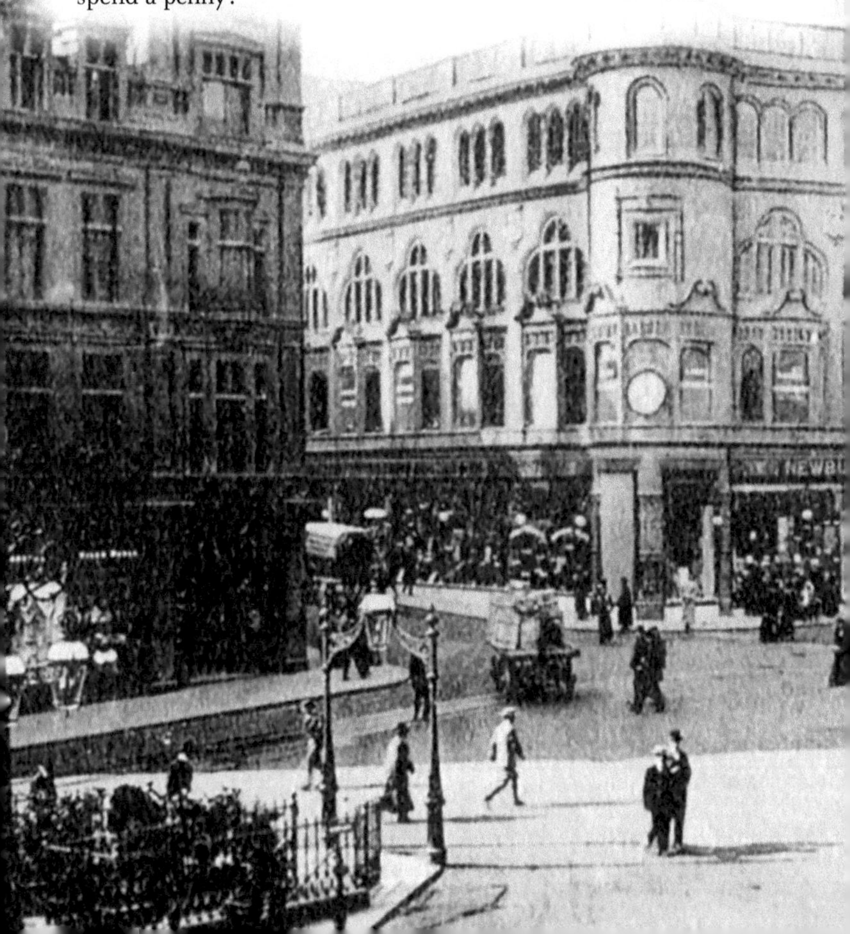

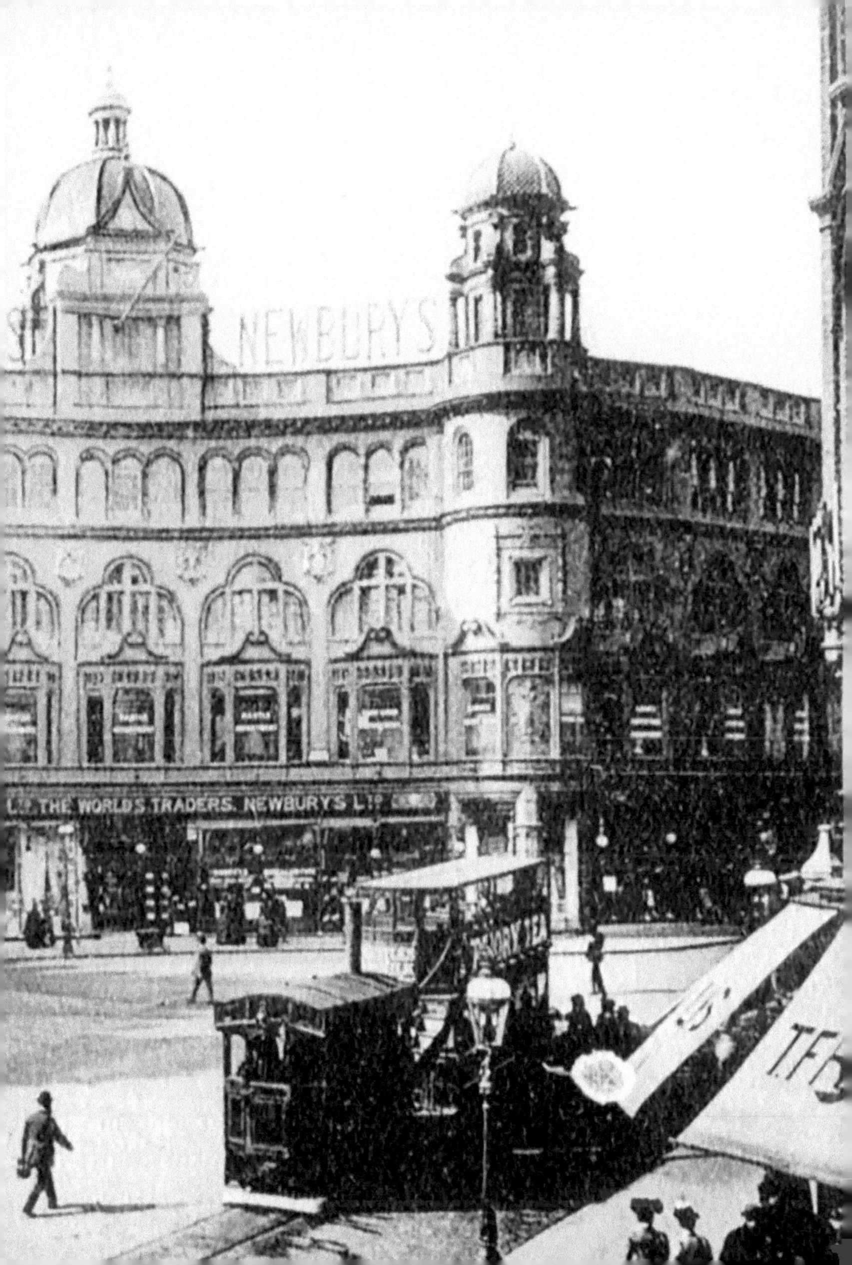

NEWBURY'S
L.TD THE WORLD'S TRADERS. NEWBURY'S L.TD
T.F.

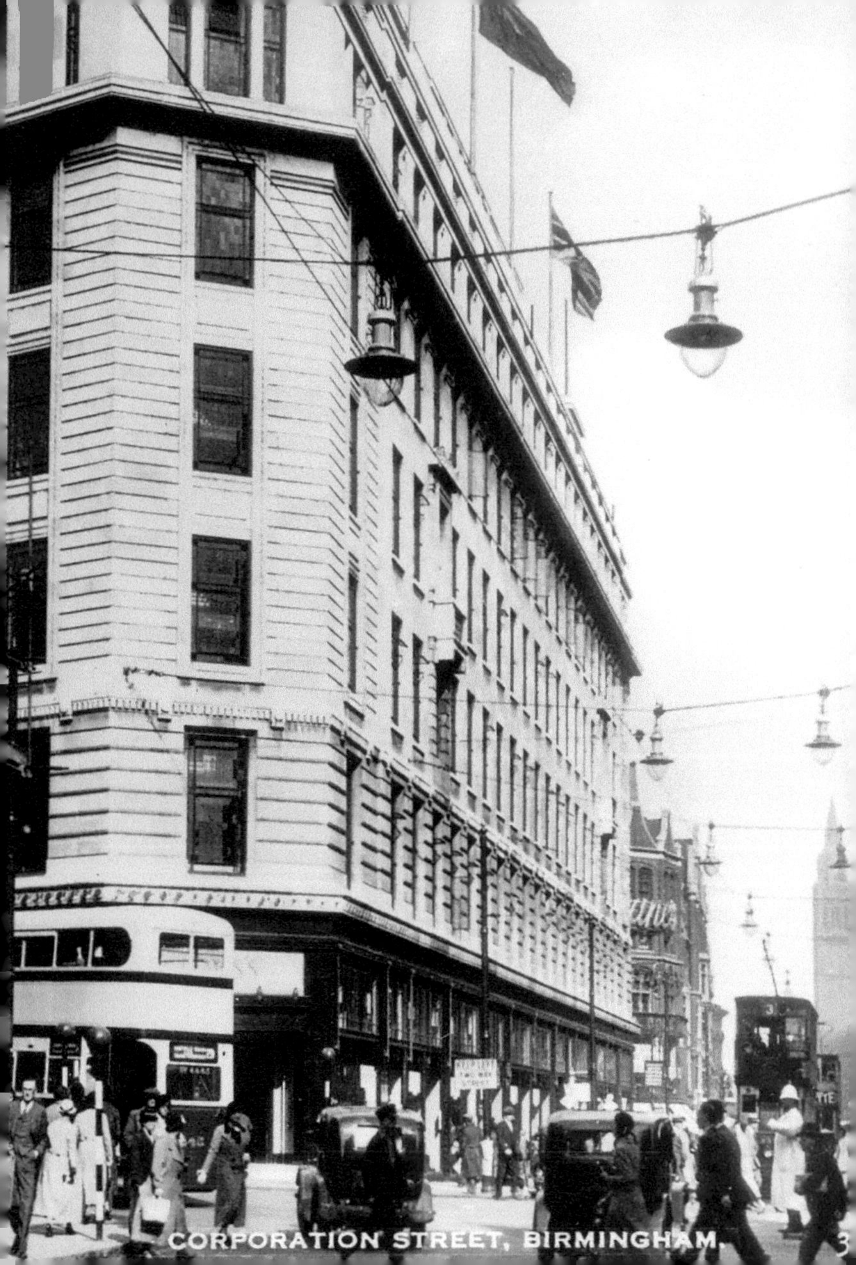

CORPORATION STREET, BIRMINGHAM.

22. LEWIS', CORPORATION STREET

'Over 200 shops in one' was the bold claim of Lewis' which became the city's largest and arguably most go-ahead store during the 1930s. Situated on the corner of Bull Street and Corporation Street, the well-placed store emphatically maintained that in addition to selling a vast range of goods, it also provided services, such as hairdressing, tickets for theatre shows, travel tickets, refreshment areas and light music.

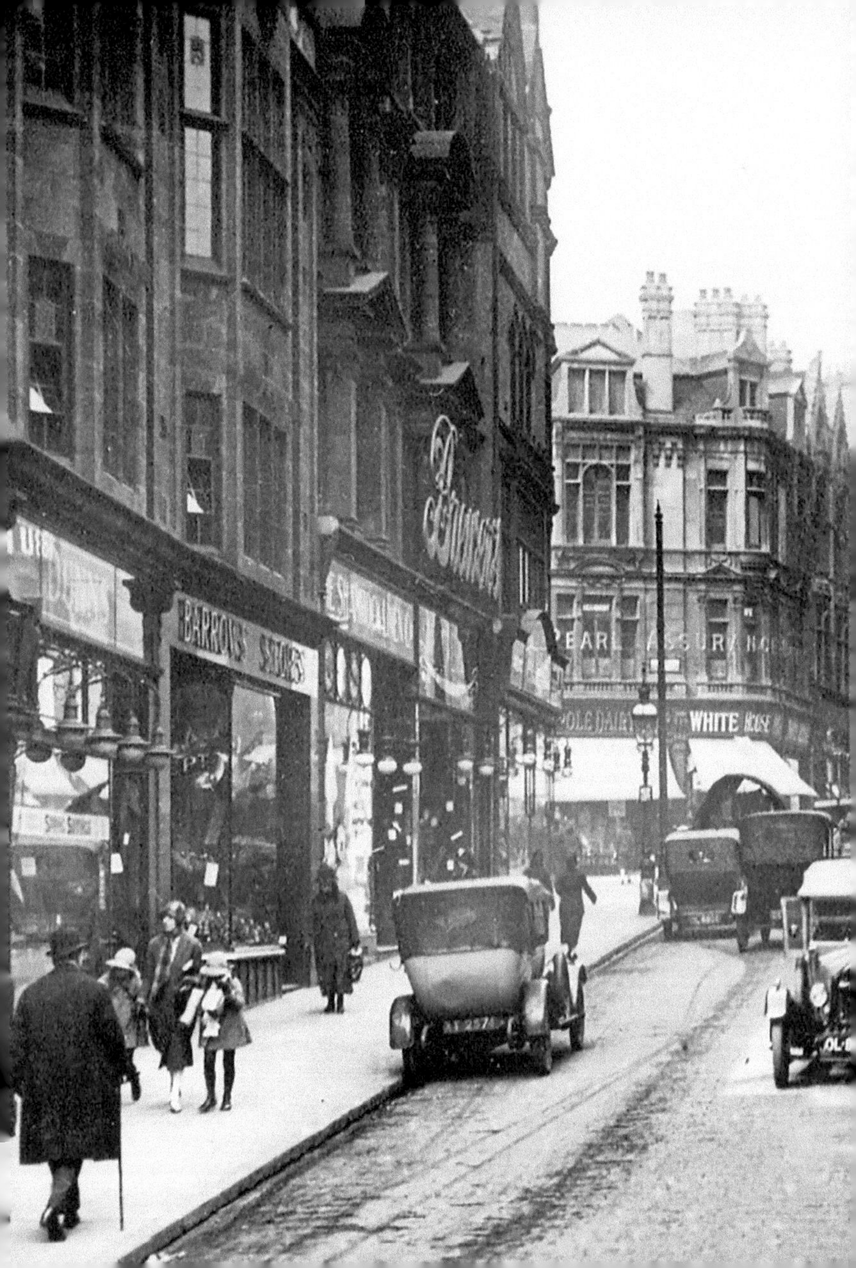

23. BULL STREET

This lower part of Bull Street is replete with shops. This image, taken between the wars, shows a number of very hat-conscious shoppers. The hats worn by men were often a pointer to their social class: flat cap denoted working class, whereas trilbies were worn by white-collar workers.

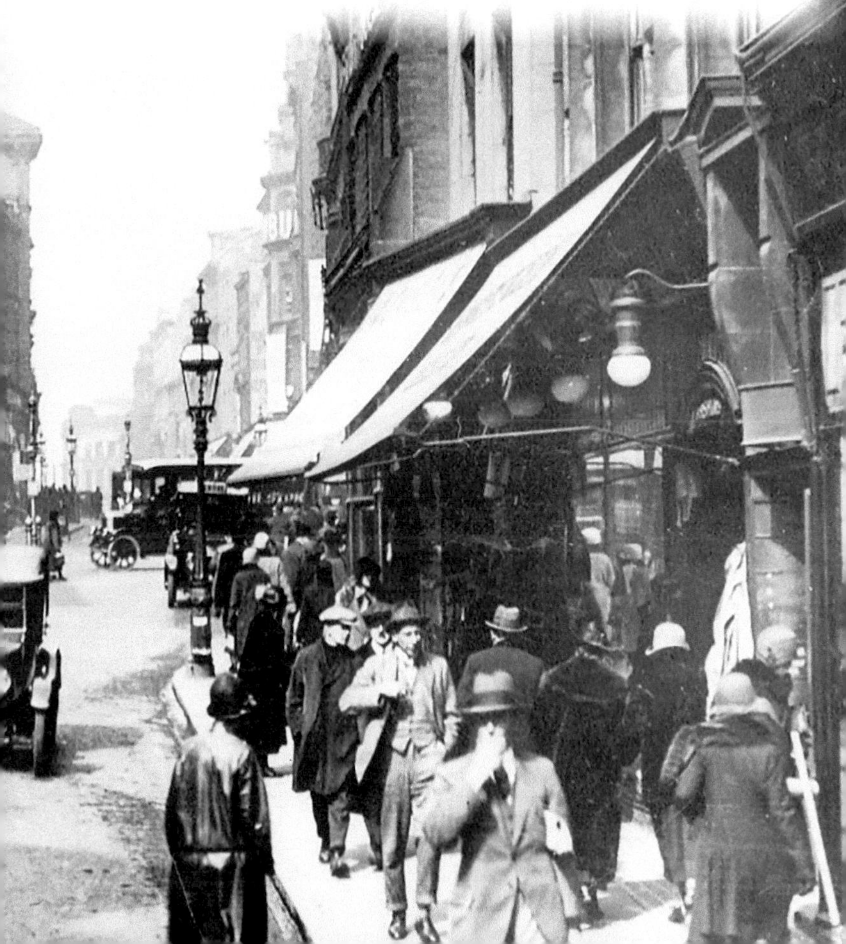

24. MARTINEAU STREET – HIGH STREET

At one time Birmingham had over thirty different tram routes. As a city terminus, Martineau Street catered for Witton (the No. 3), Washwood Heath (No. 10), Perry Barr (No. 6), and Alum Rock (No. 8). The low building behind the second tram is the News Theatre, which became the first cinema of its kind to be established in the provinces when it opened in 1932.

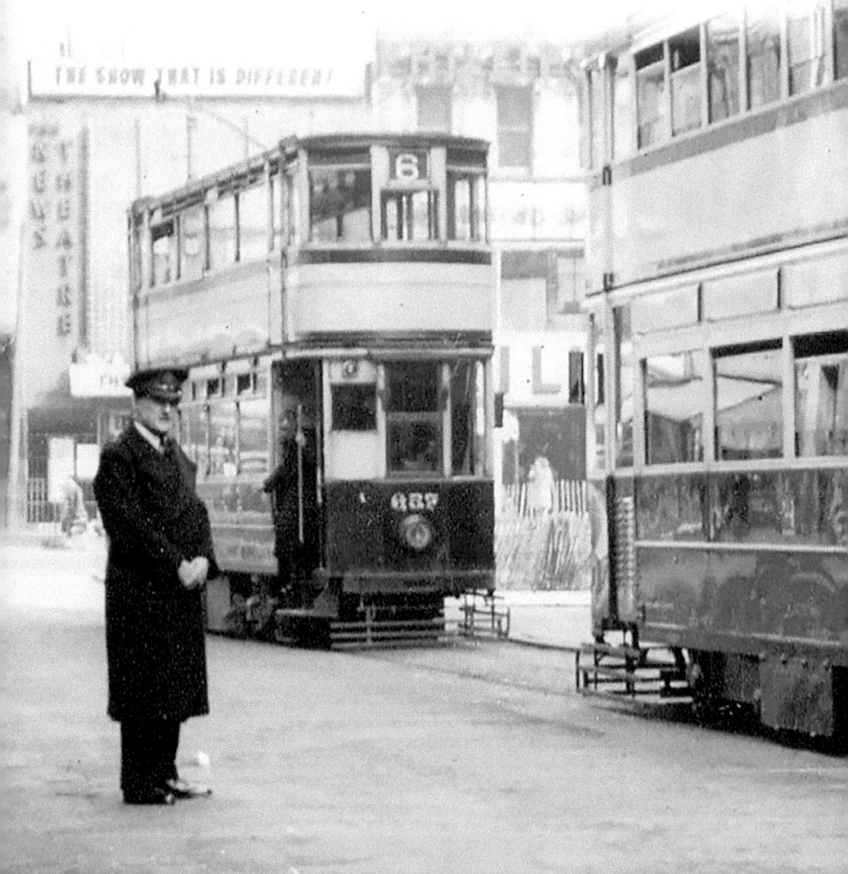

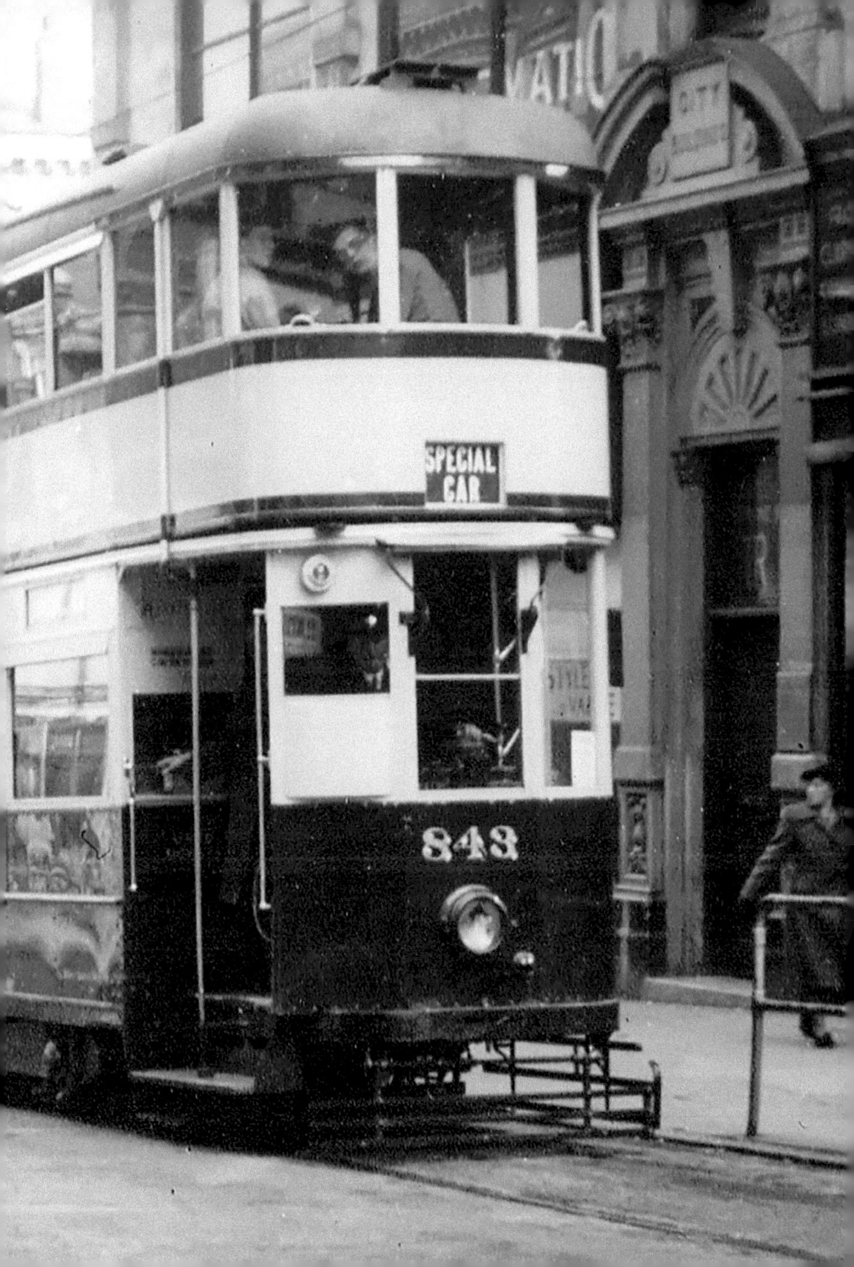

VATIC
CITY
SPECIAL
CAR
843

25. HIGH STREET

As in many cities, Turkish baths were in vogue and to be found in High Street. A vertical advertising sign can be seen just right of the entrance to the Midland Arcade.

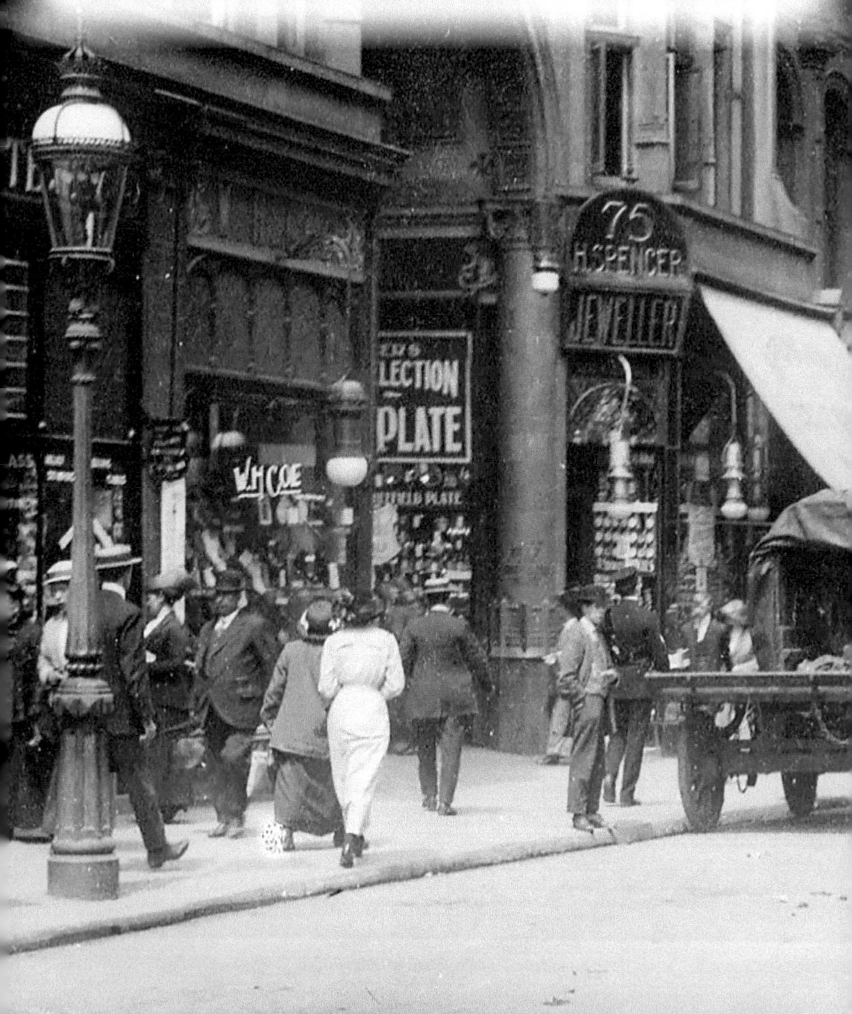

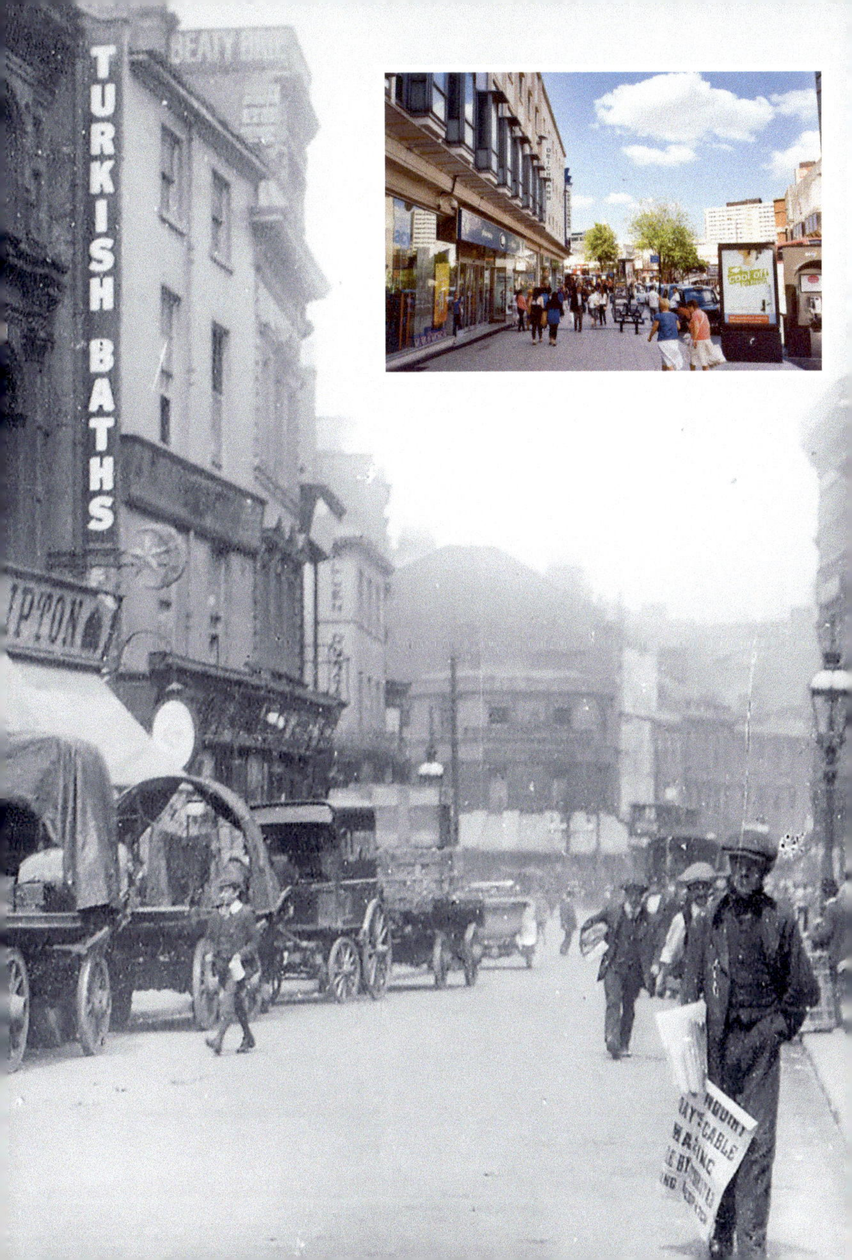

TURKISH BATS
TURKISH BATHS
BEATY BROS
LIPTON

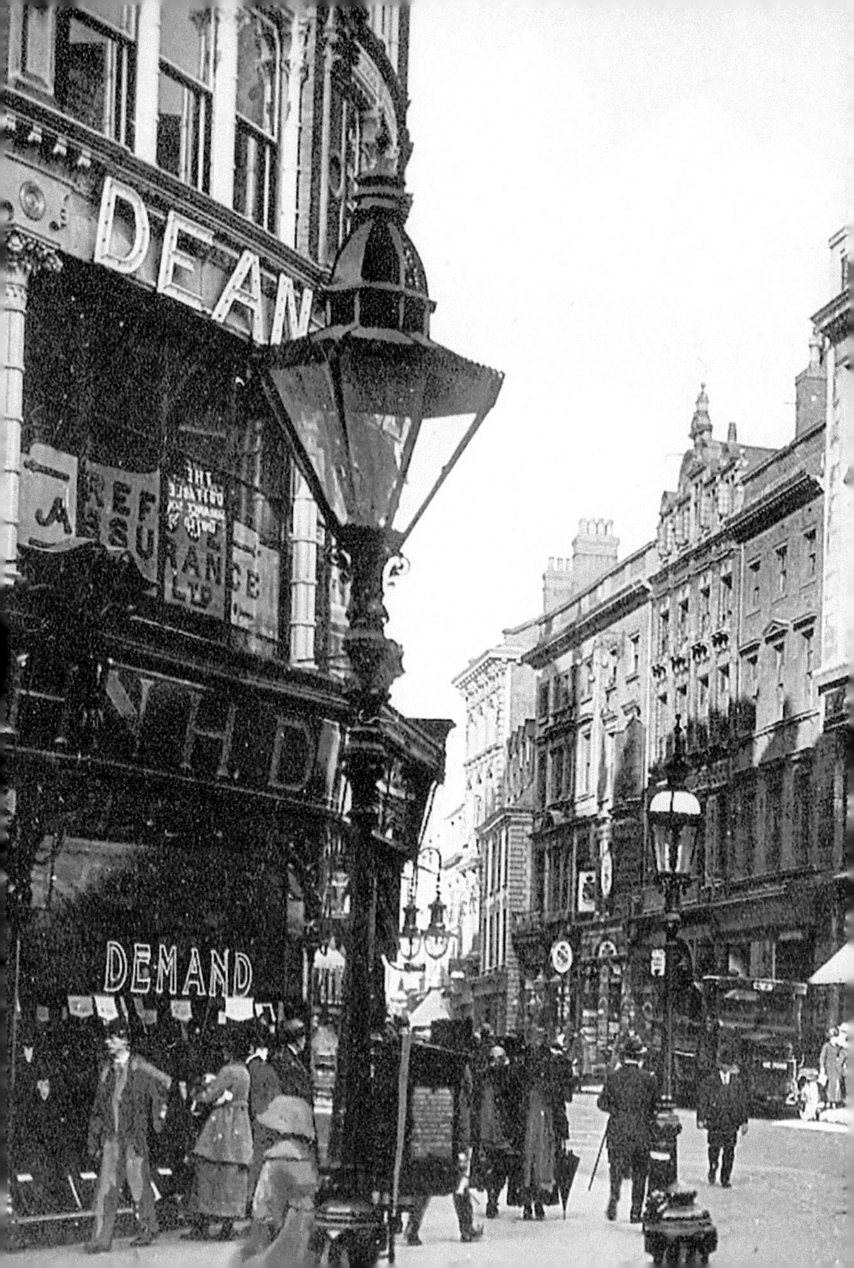
DEAN
FREE
ASSURANCE
N H D
DEMAND

26. HIGH STREET – NEW STREET

Moving towards the Bull Ring, High Street continues to the right, with New Street opening on the left. Above the lower shop blind 'Foster Brothers' can be read, a well-known multiple men's clothing firm. Above the awnings on the left 'Co-operative Society' is just visible – the headquarters of the 'biggest trader in town'.

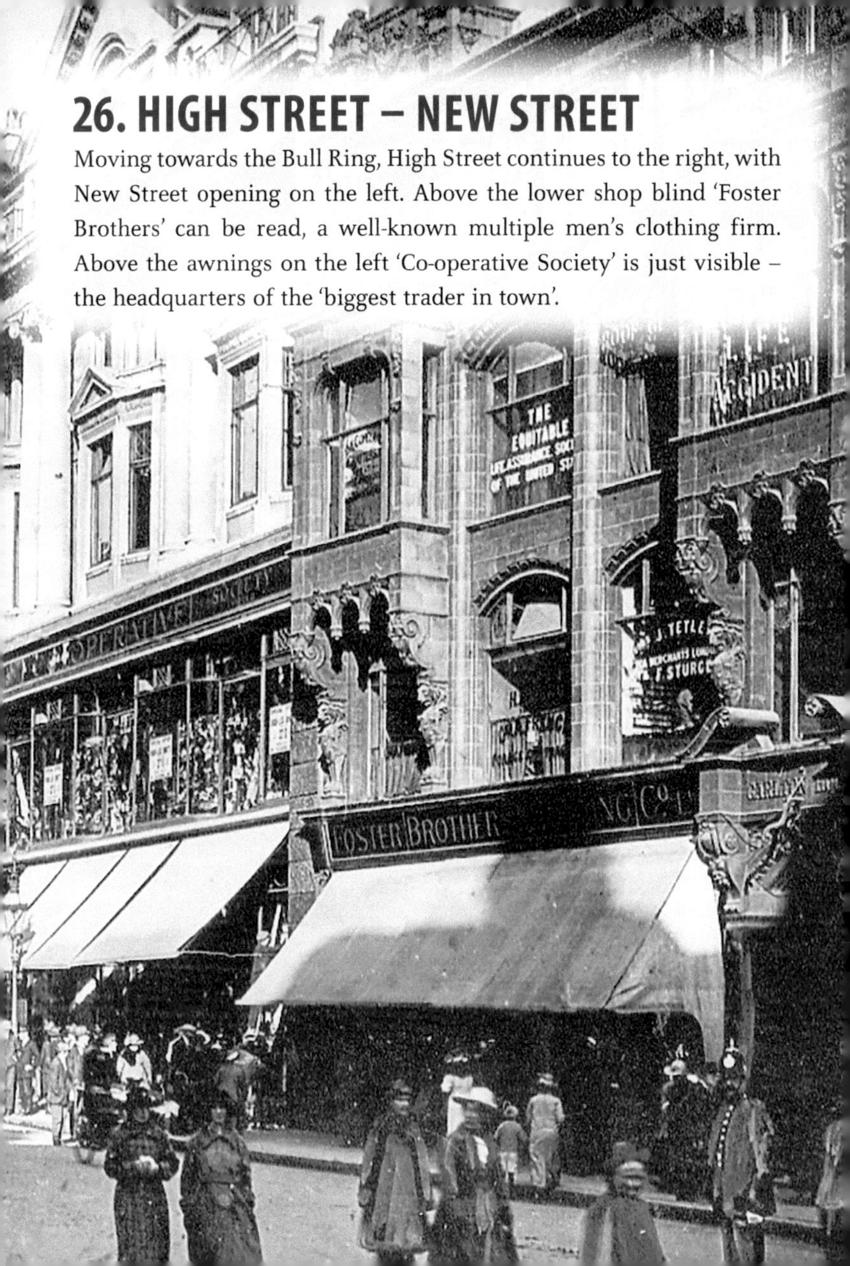

27. THE BULL RING

For Brummies, the greatest magnet of the city centre was once the Bull Ring. A good choice of stalls were available in the open and many more were inside the iconic Market Hall – a building destroyed by fire in a 1940 air raid. Amid the bustle and banter, occasional quack medicine men and political orators all sold their wares. There is lots of hustle and more bustle today – an interesting and entertaining place to be.

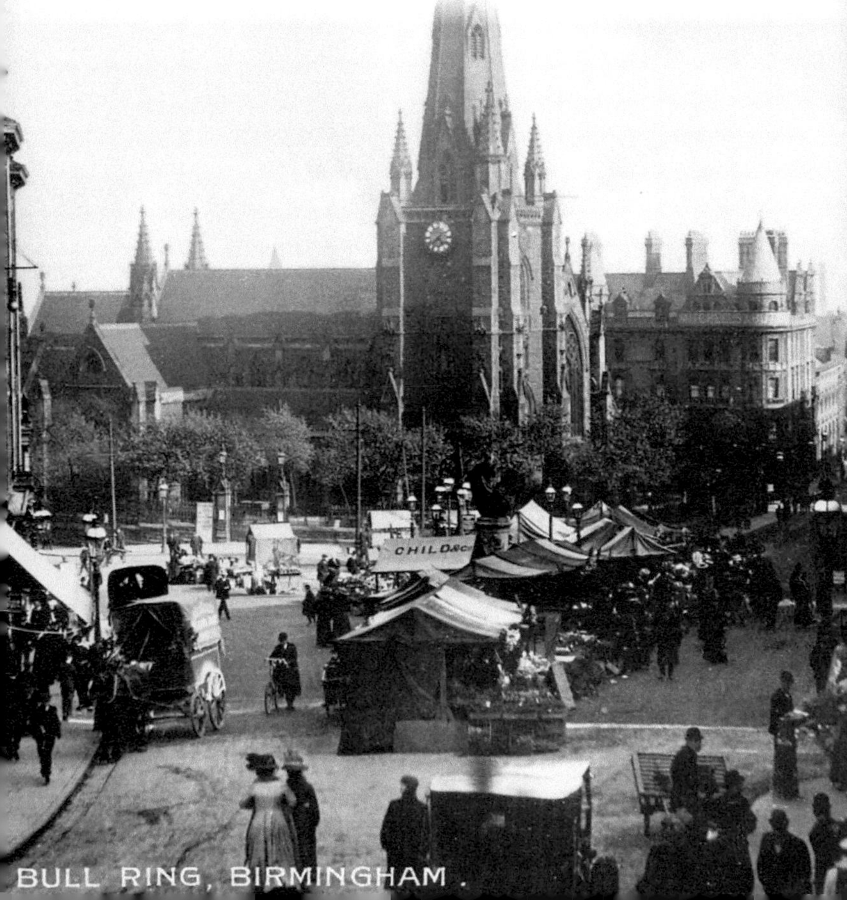

28. ST MARTIN'S CHURCH, BULL RING

Several much earlier churches preceded St Martin's, which was consecrated in 1875. For many years it was known as the 'church in the market'. While it remains in the market area, its earlier prominence in the Bull Ring now seems rather hemmed in.

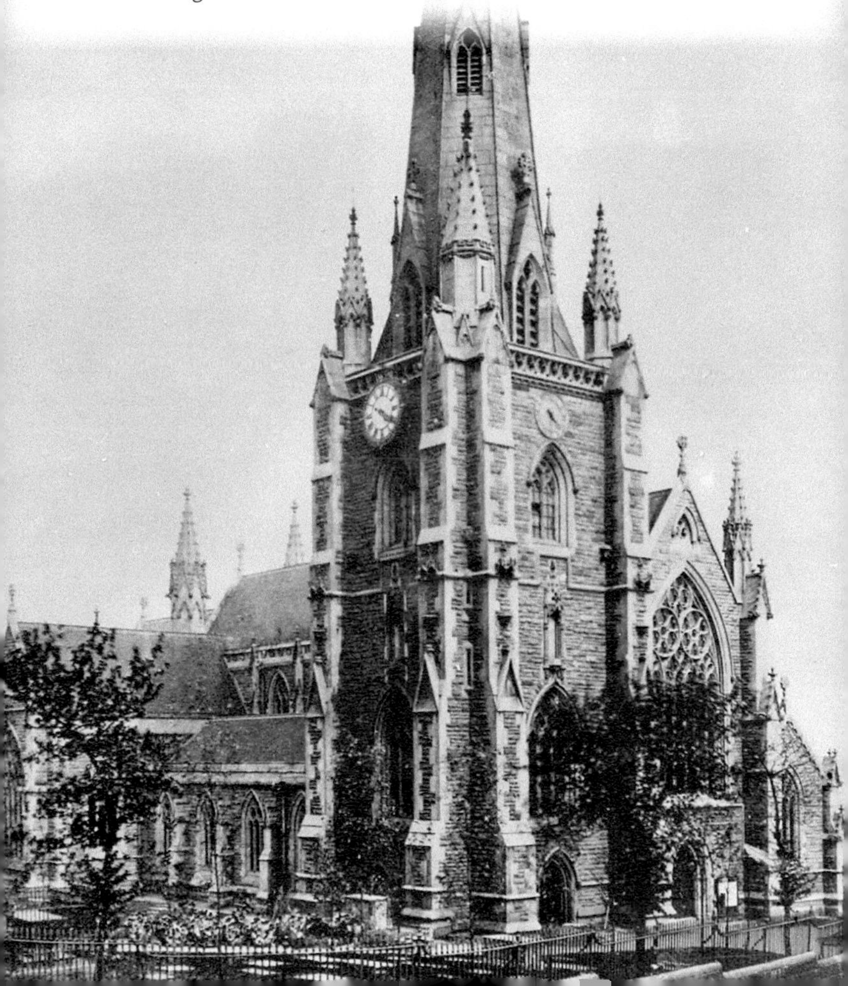

29. OPEN MARKET, BULL RING

This image offers a closer look at the fruit and veg in the outdoor market, with the impressive statue of Lord Nelson keeping watch. It is reputed that Birmingham was the first British town to honour Nelson by public subscription.

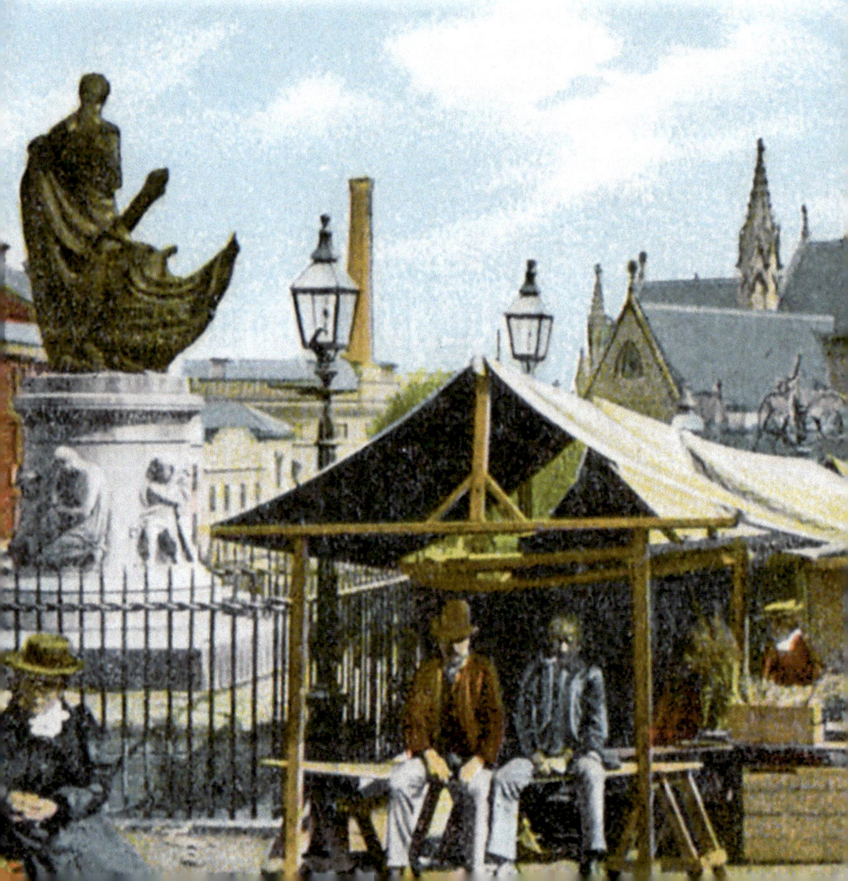

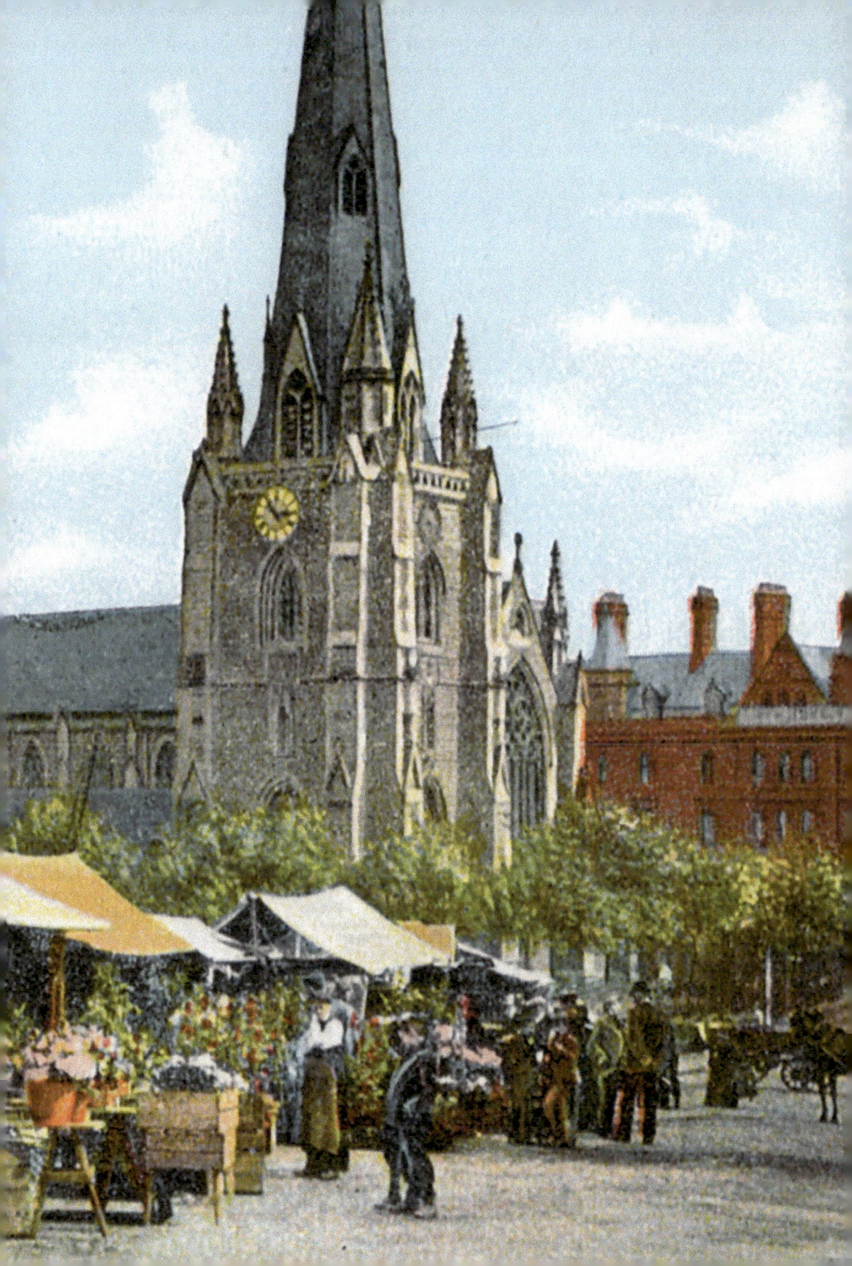

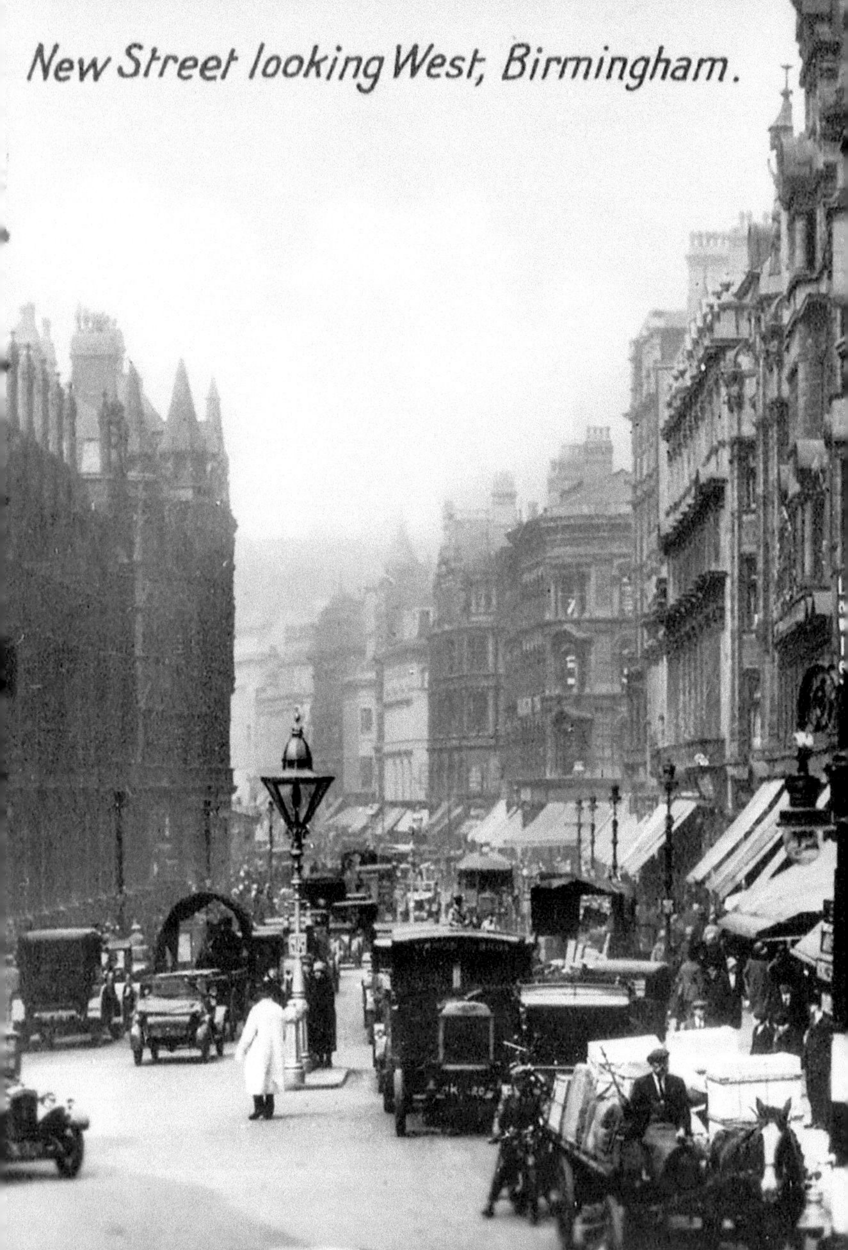

New Street looking West, Birmingham.

30. NEW STREET EAST I

If you return to New Street via Nelson's new plinth, you'll enter the eastern section of New Street which is shown here as being chock-a-block with commercial and shopping activities. Horse-drawn wagons, visible in this image, were commonplace delivery vehicles working from railway goods yards. The white-coated traffic policeman had also become a regular sight at this time.

31. NEW STREET EAST II

Further along, on the site of the Hen and Chickens coaching inn, a temperance hotel named the Arden was built. This closed in 1972. Next door, the Paramount cinema, seating well over 2,000 people, opened in 1937 with a dashing Errol Flynn in the swashbuckling *Charge of the Light Brigade.*

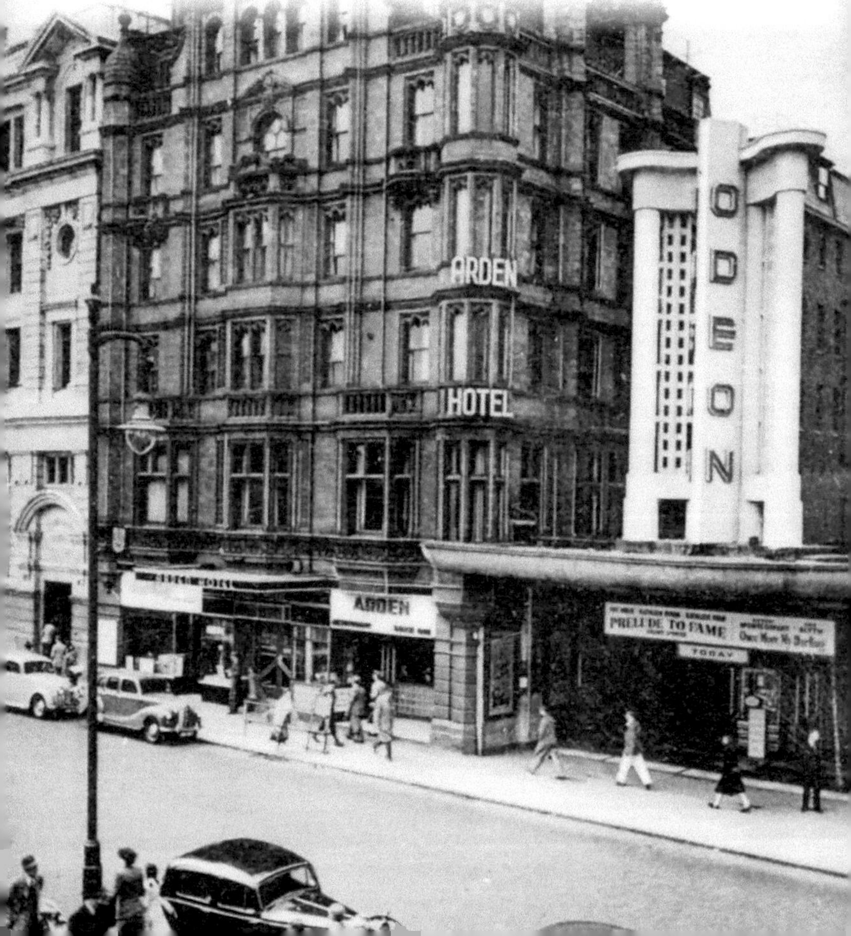

32. CORPORATION STREET – NEW STREET

This image is looking along Corporation Street from where east and west New Street join. The postcard, franked 1917, shows the start of the 'boulevard' dear to Joseph Chamberlain's heart. Acres of slums have been cleared away from this area.

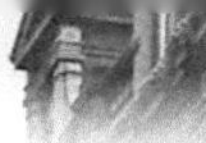

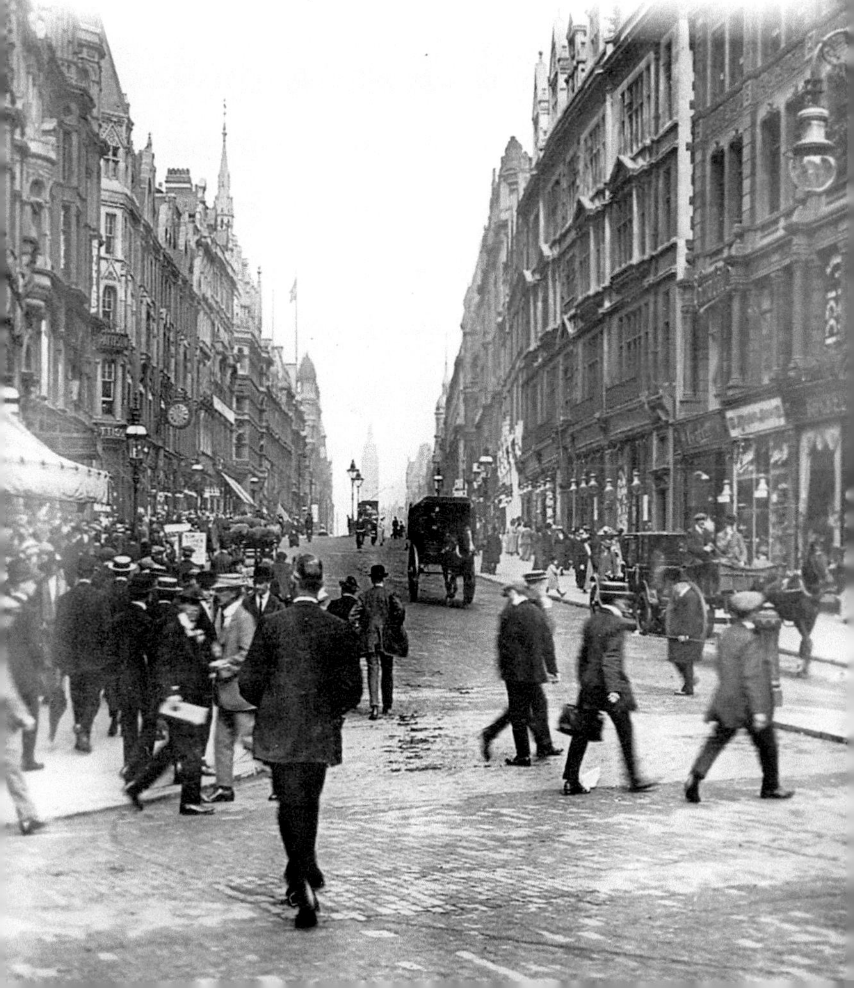

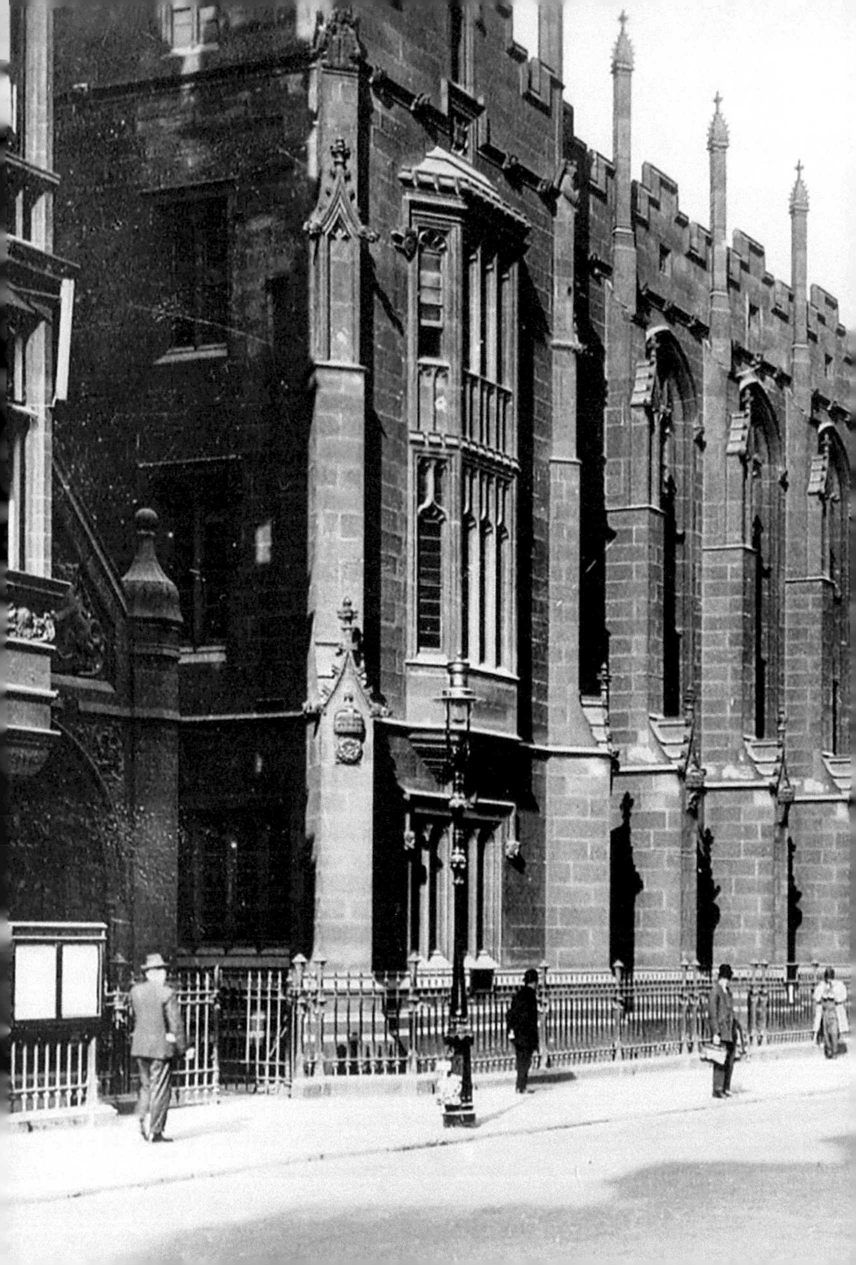

33. NEW STREET EAST III

This building, designed by Sir Charles Barry, architect of the Palace of Westminster in London, was opened in 1833 as the top school in Birmingham for boys. The building was demolished in 1936, the new boys' school is now in a modern building on Bristol Road.

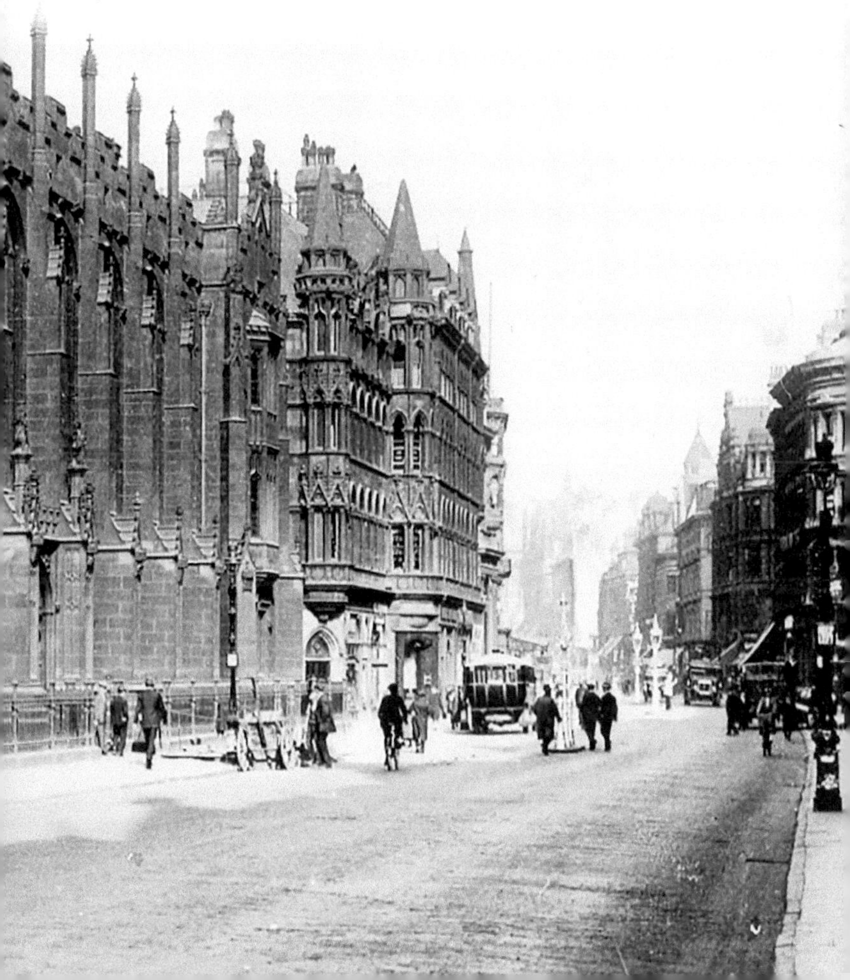

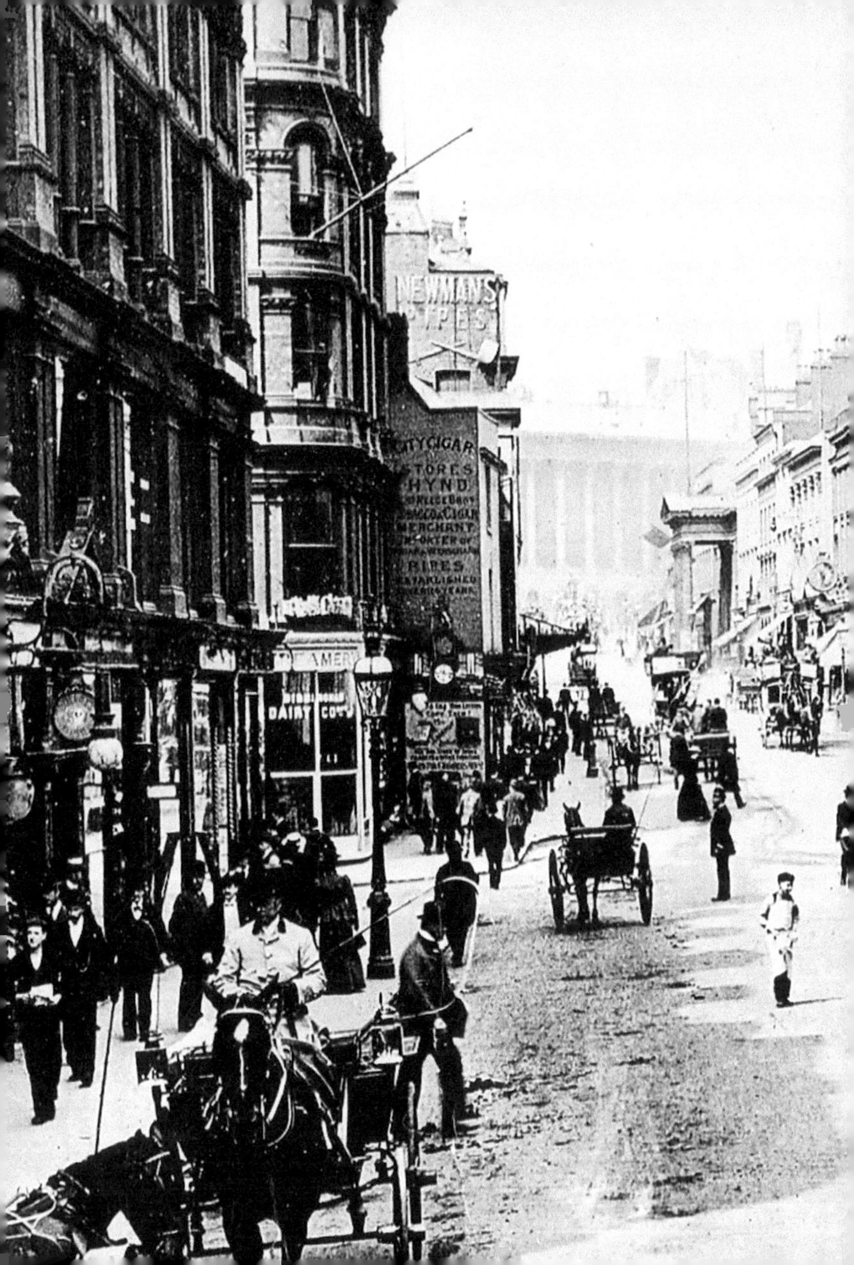

NEWMANS
PIPES
CITY CIGAR
STORES
HYND
TOBACCO & CIGAR
MERCHANT
PIPES
CREAMERY
DAIRY CO

34. NEW STREET WEST I

The postcard in this image has been franked 1904, when horse power was very much in control. A horse bus can be seen to the right and at the bottom left is a coachman in uniform, holding the reins of a fine carriage. This street was home to the Theatre Royal (demolished in 1956). The portico to the right, fronted a hall housing paintings (demolished in 1912).

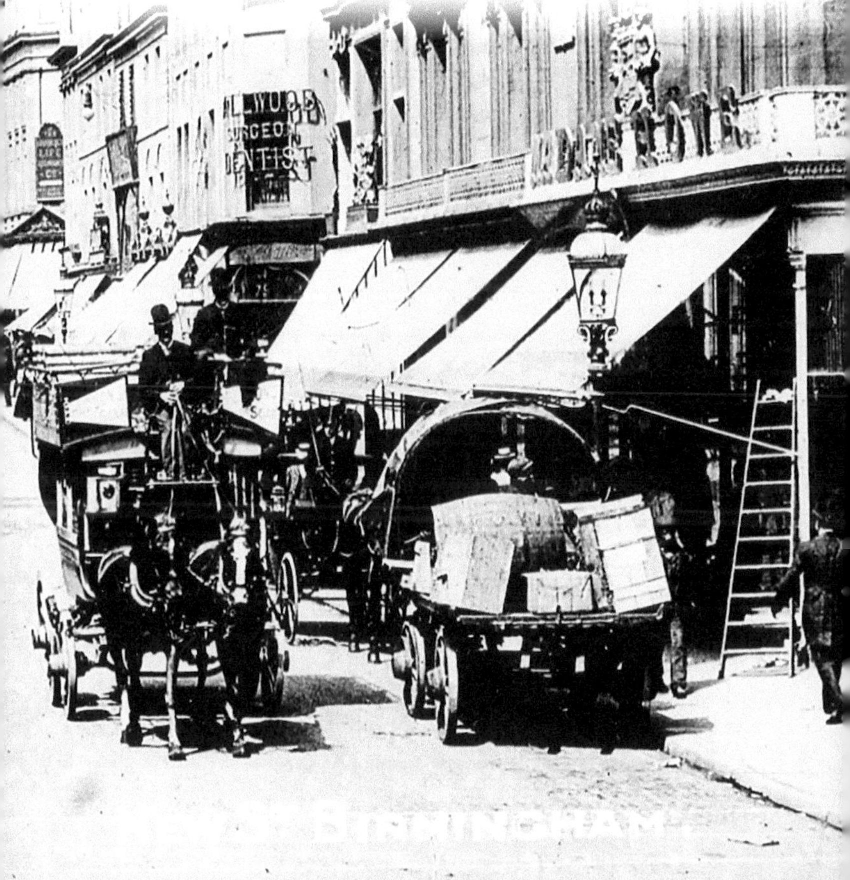

35. NEW STREET WEST II

Points of interest in this section of New Street include the town hall in the distance. In this image, the lorry by the lights is about to turn into Stephenson Place. Above the traffic lights on the right stands the premises of *Birmingham Post and Mail*, a major provincial newspaper.

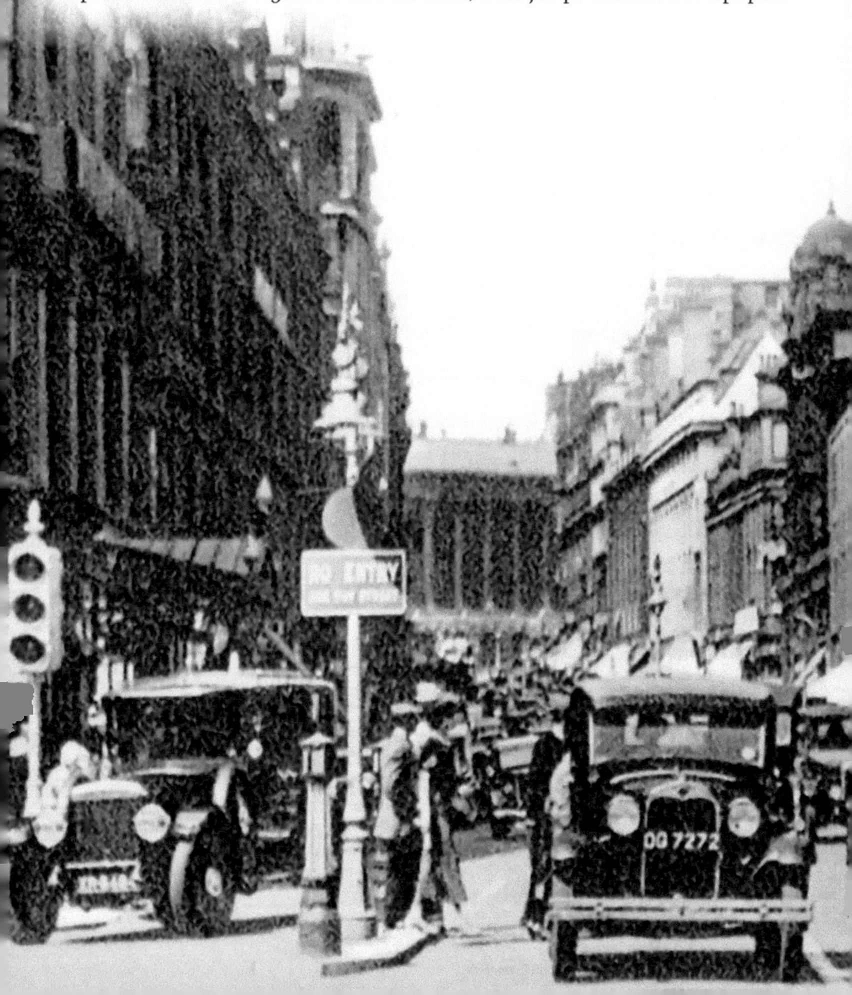

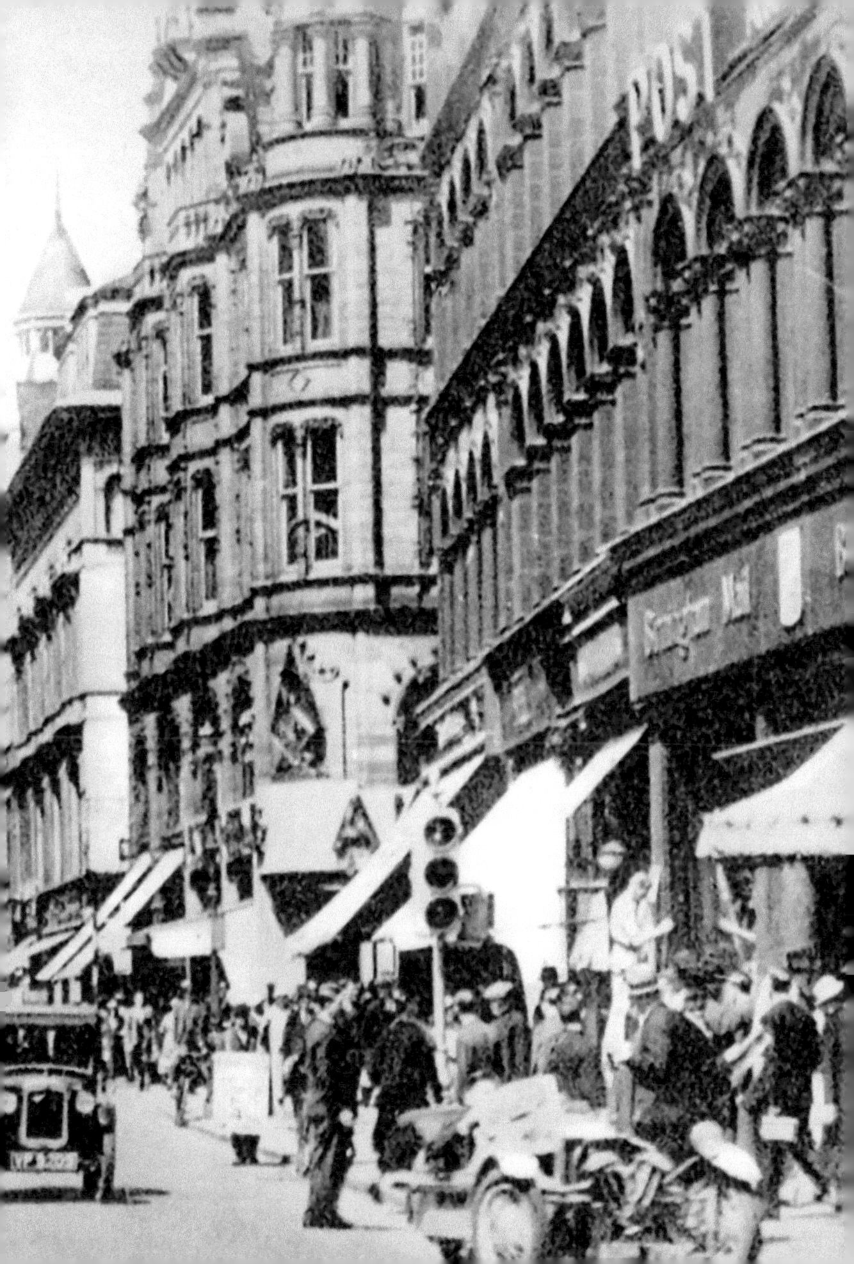

36. NEW STREET STATION

This image, still from the time of steam trains, offers a fine panoramic view. The two parts of the station are separated by Queens Drive. This station has been completely overhauled quite recently and includes a John Lewis which forms part of the massive shopping area known as Grand Central.

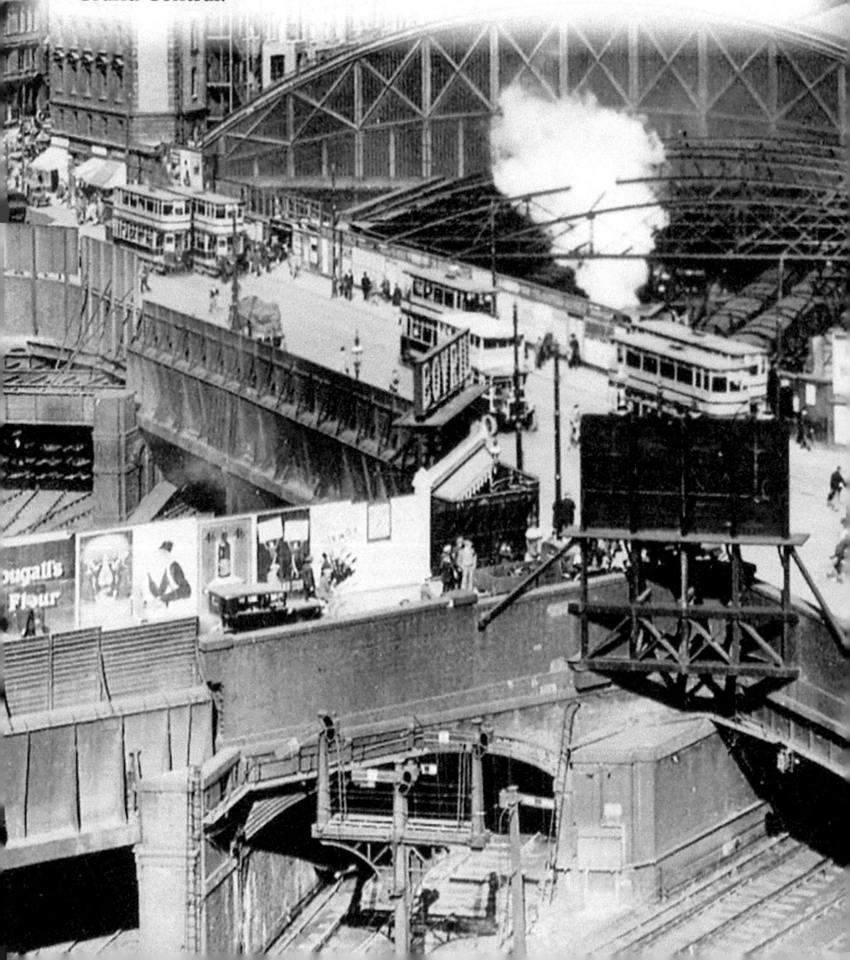

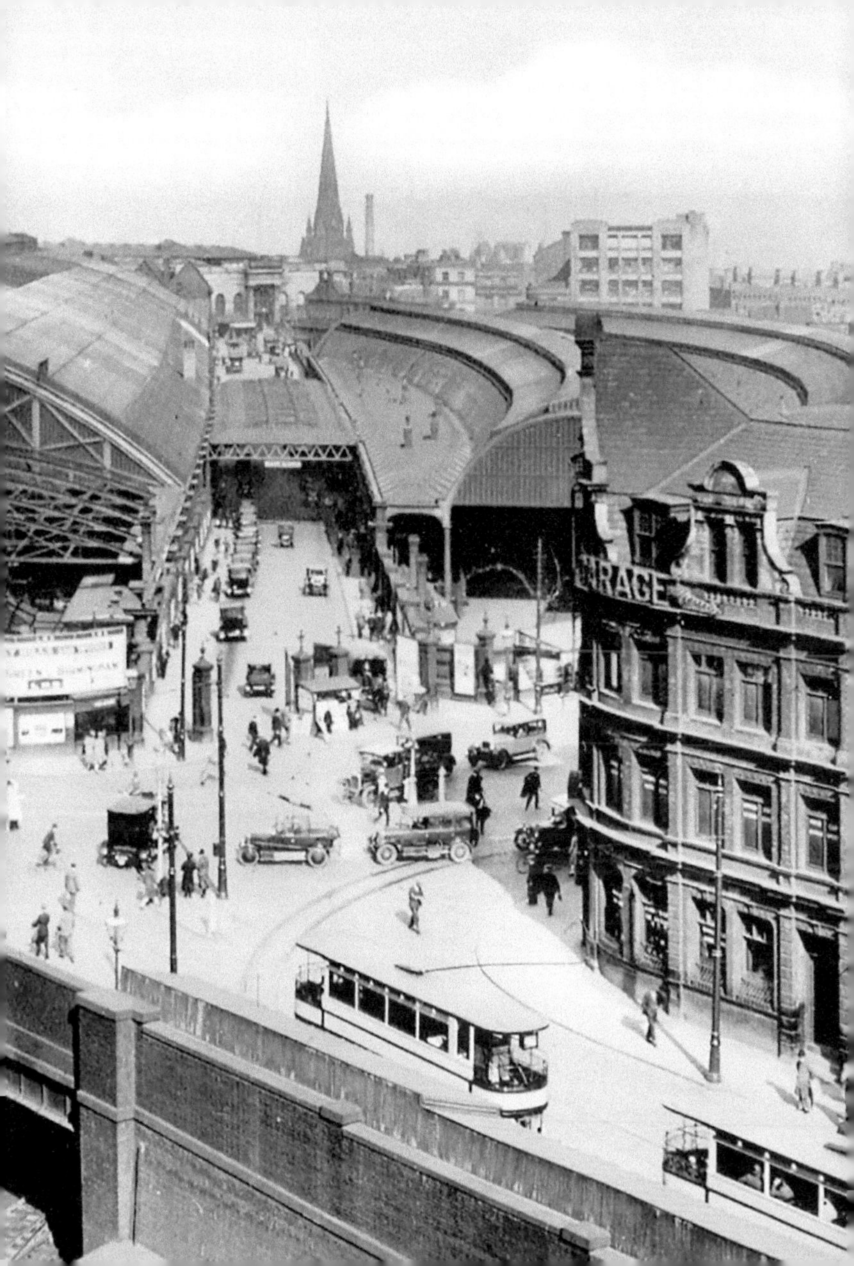

37. NAVIGATION STREET

The Belisha beacon, its globe visible to the right of the traffic policeman's helmet, indicates that this scene dates to no earlier than 1934, when such safety beacons were introduced. A number of tram routes began from this street. Service No. 35, shown here, ran to to Selly Oak (during rush periods only).

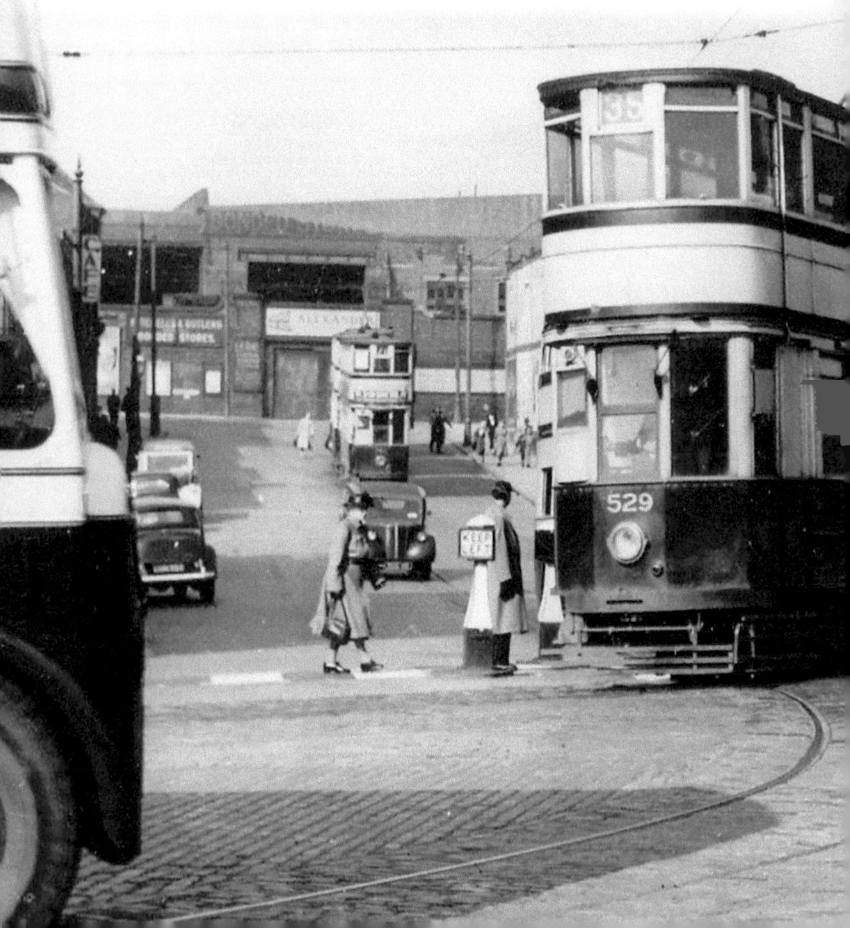

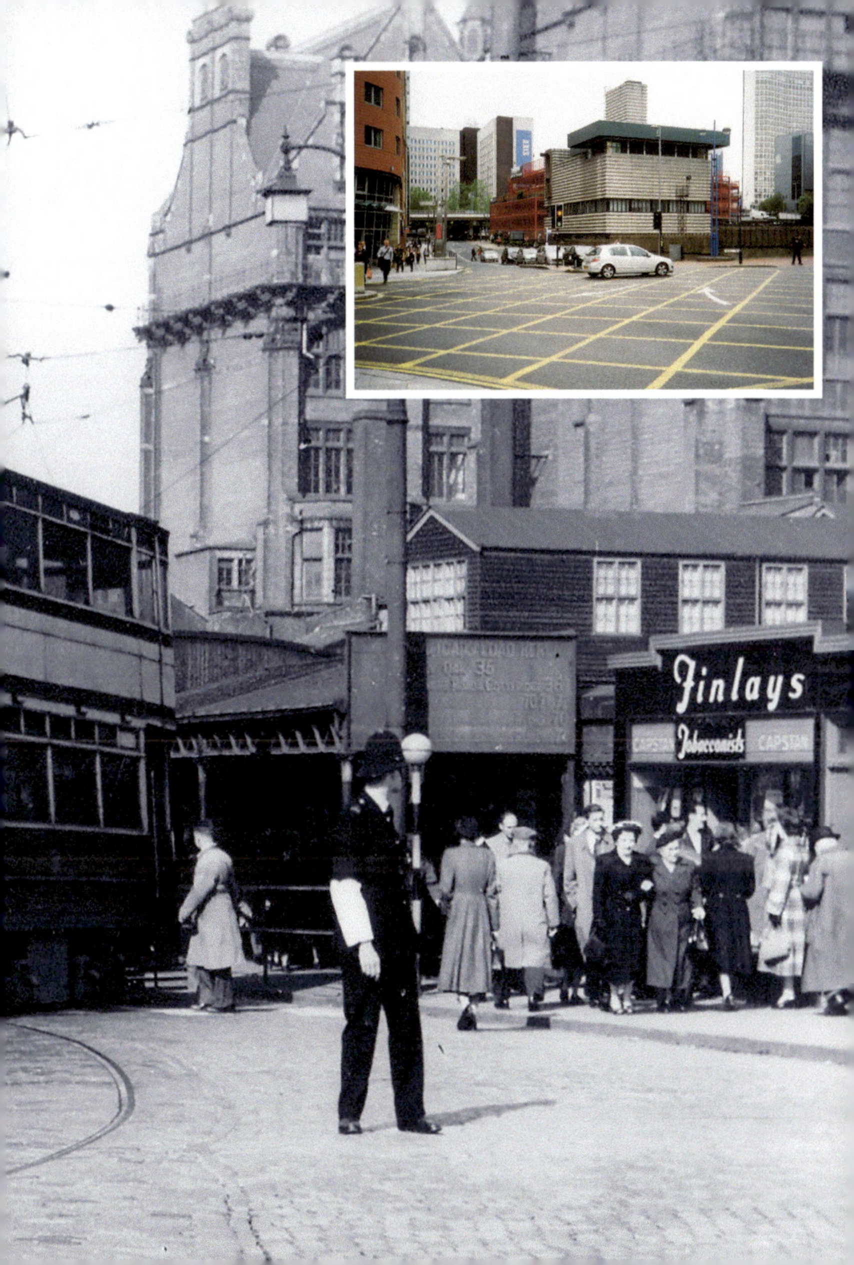
Finlays
Tobacconists
CAPSTAN
CAPSTAN

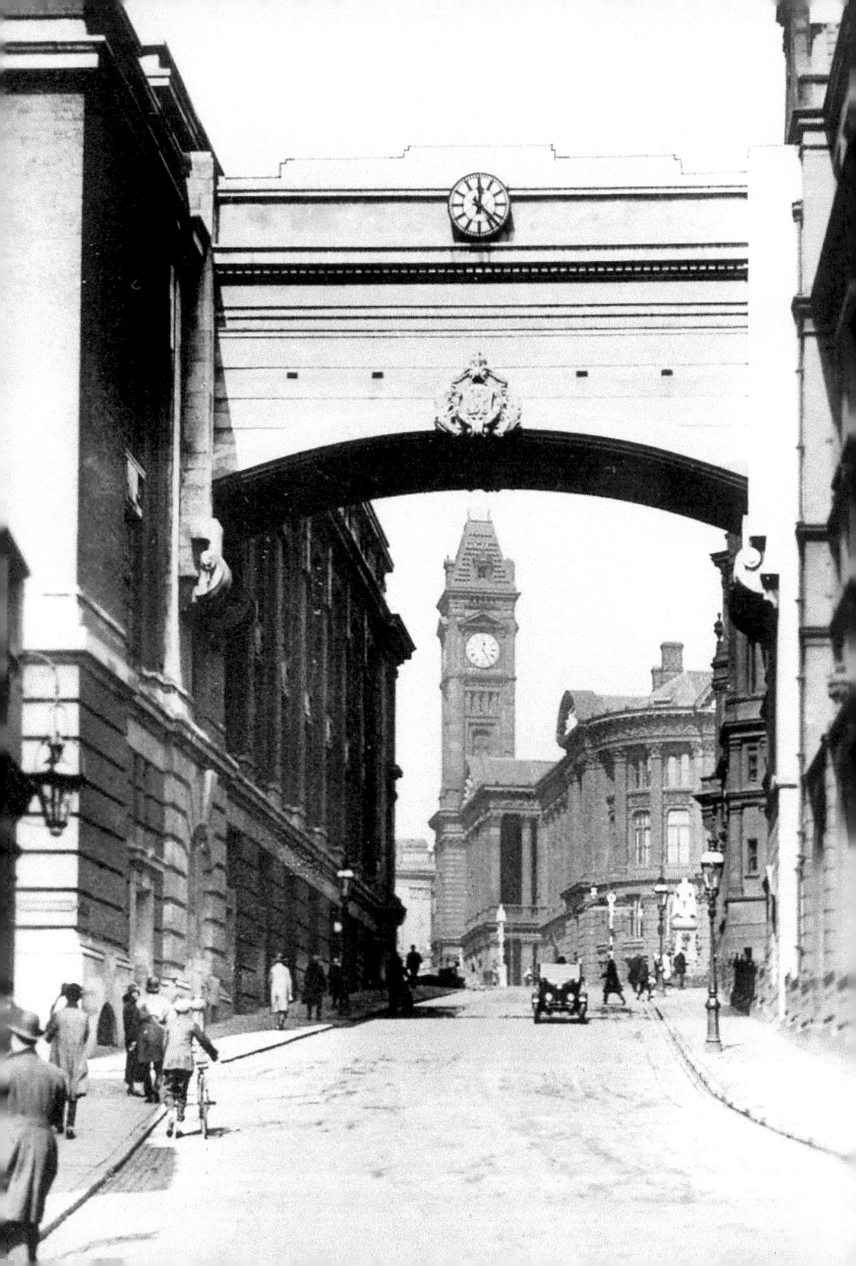

38. HILL STREET

This bridge joins two Royal Mail buildings: the head post office (right) and the parcel office in Hill Street (left). By chance perhaps, the bridge added interest to an ordinary sort of street and provided a more photogenic view of the Council House and the city's 'Big Ben'.

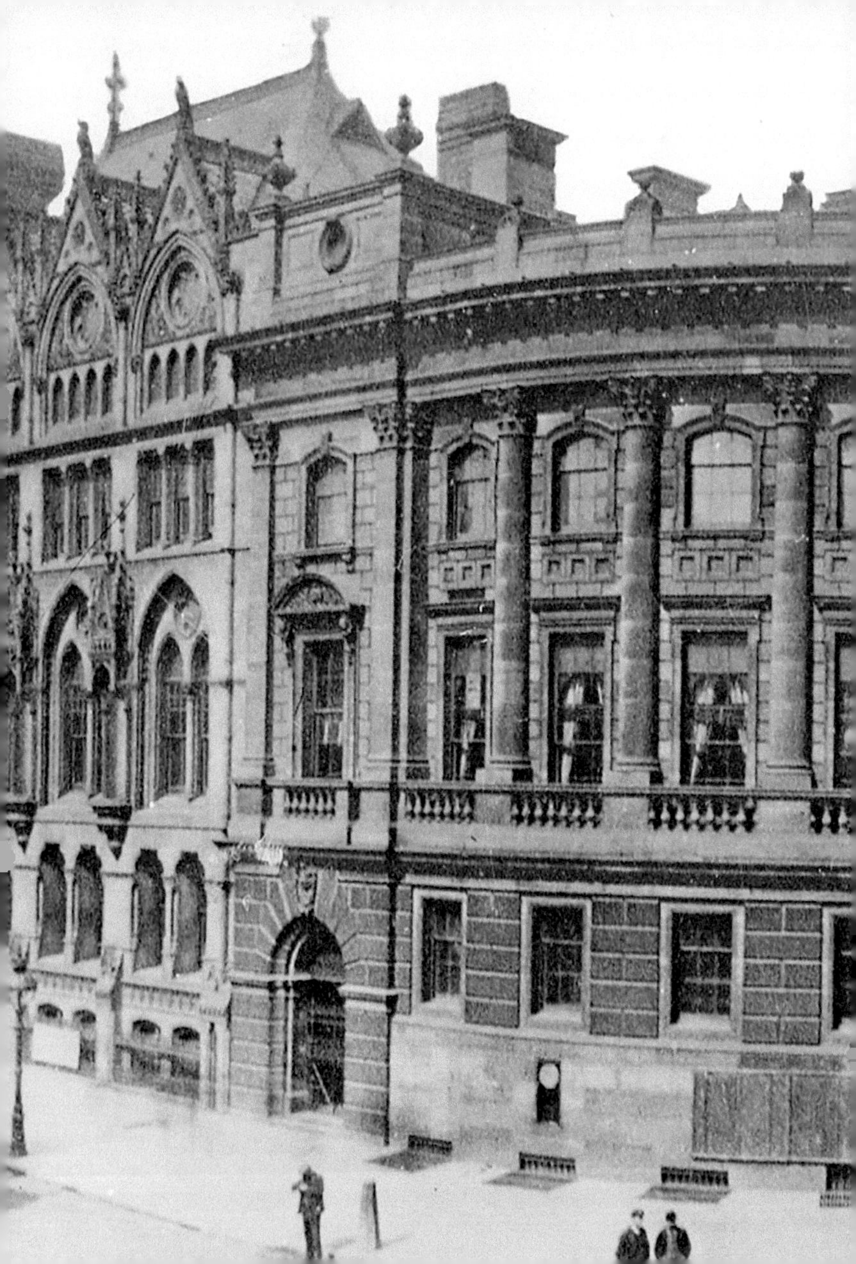

39. PARADISE STREET I

This building on the corner of Ratcliff Place and Paradise Street was known as the Midland Institute. It opened in 1856 and had the backing of the council. The Institute zealously promoted adult education and the teaching of music received particular emphasis. This building was demolished in 1965.

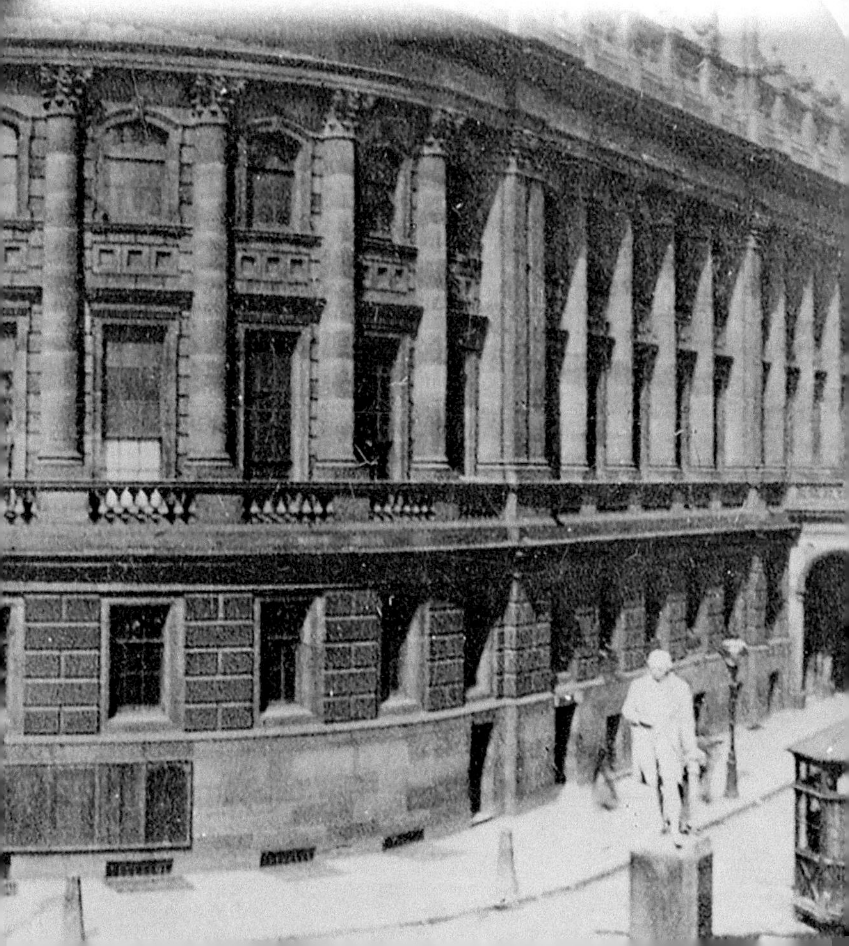

40. PARADISE STREET II

Outside the 'institutes', the workaday world carries on in this image. The horse bus can be seen on its way to New Street and other horse-drawn traffic of various kinds are on the move. Four men, possibly road repairers, are taking a break, with one of them sitting on an upturned bucket.

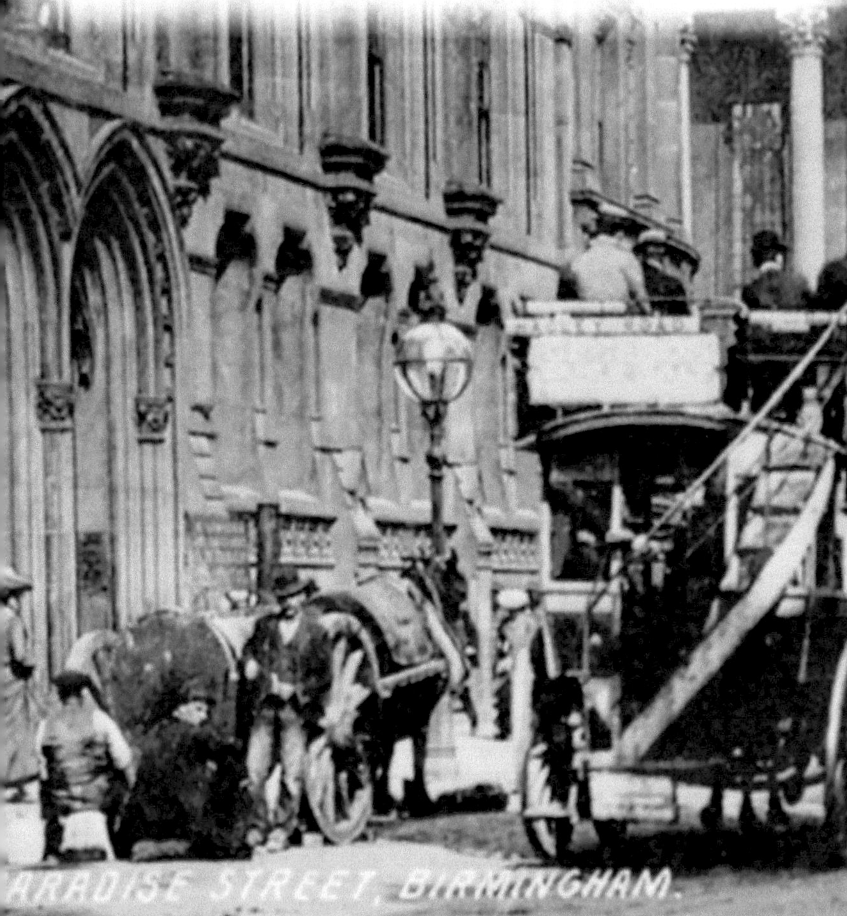

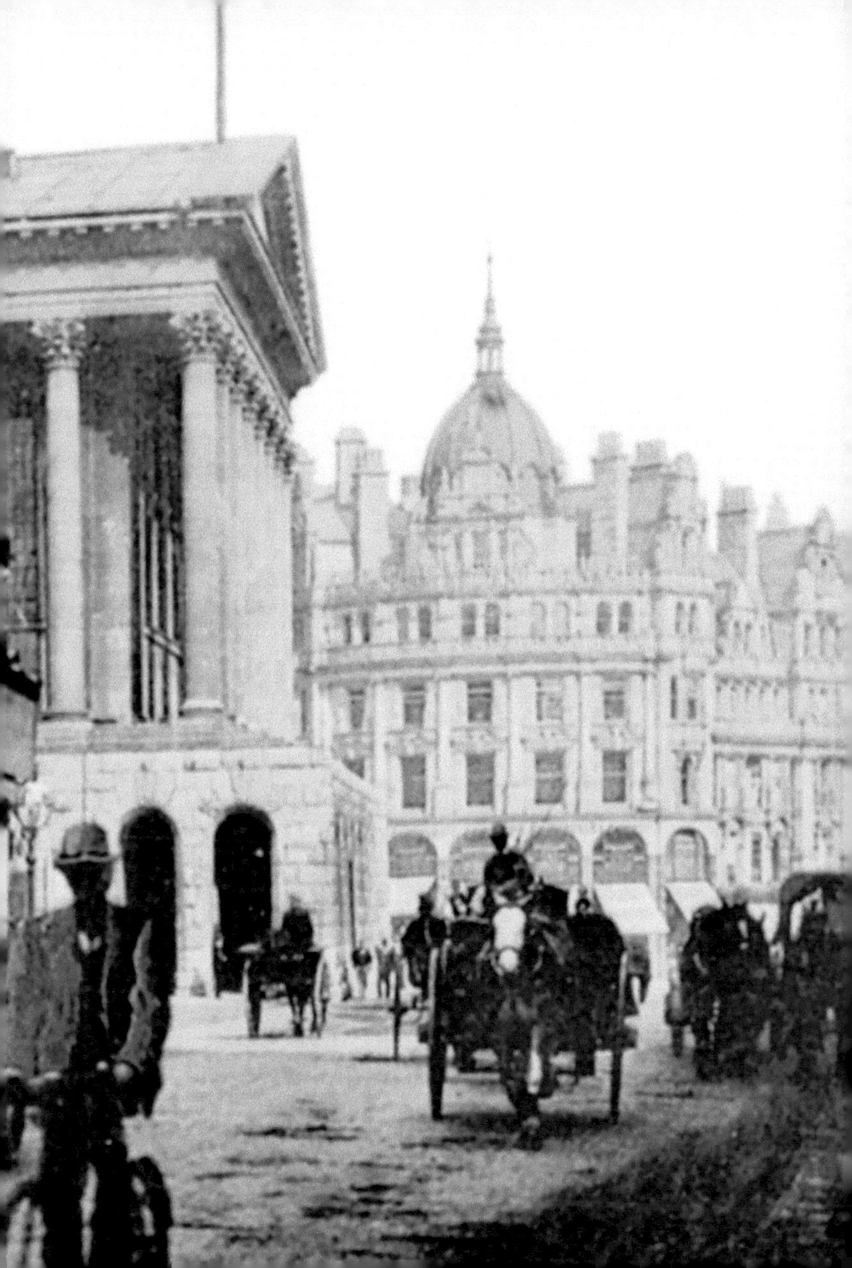

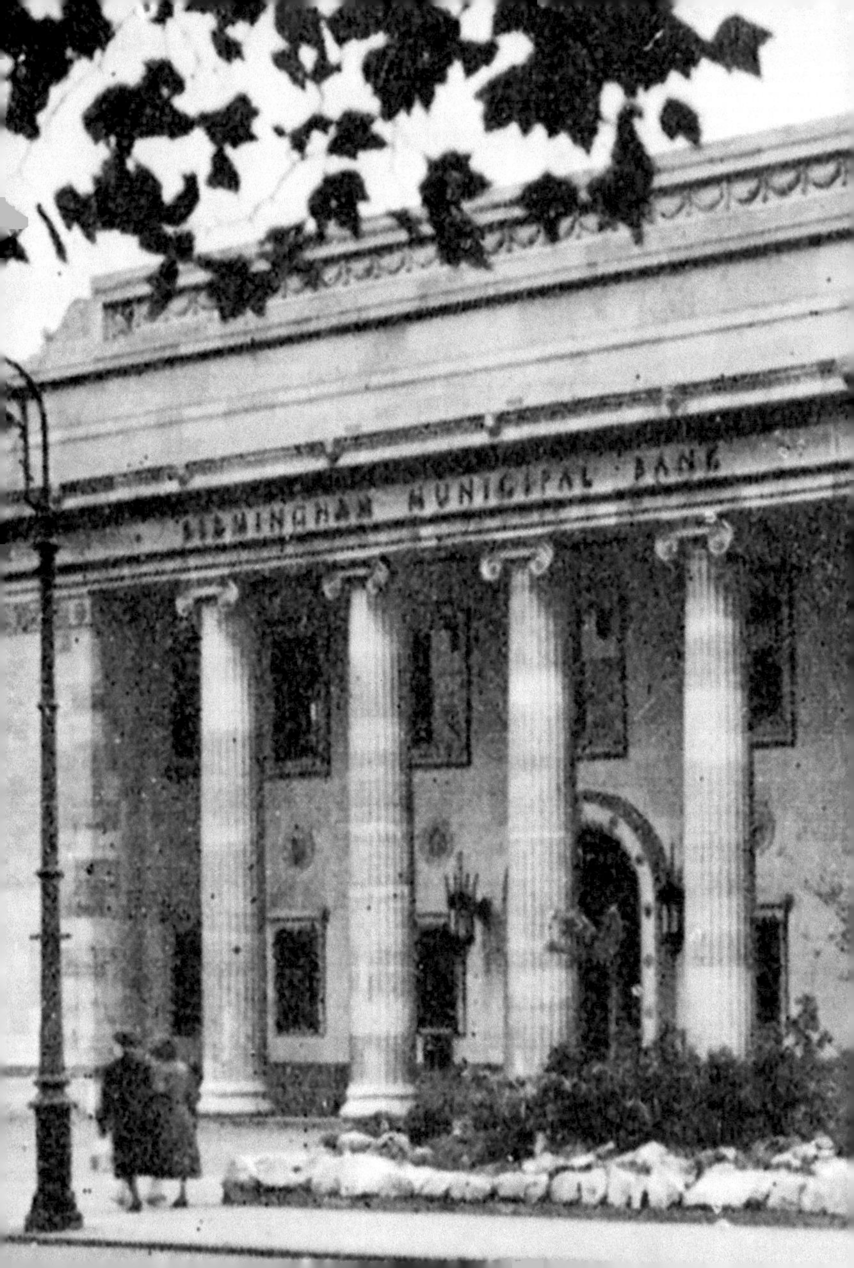
BIRMINGHAM MUNICIPAL BANK

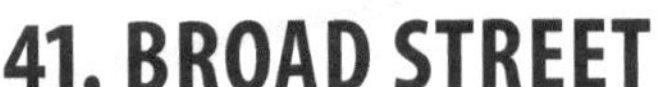

41. BROAD STREET

On we go to the bankers of Broad Street, specifically to the new head office of a bank founded in 1916 as a savings bank and to help the First World War. This current building, opened in 1933, and was strongly supported by the future prime minister Neville Chamberlain, son of Joseph Chamberlain.

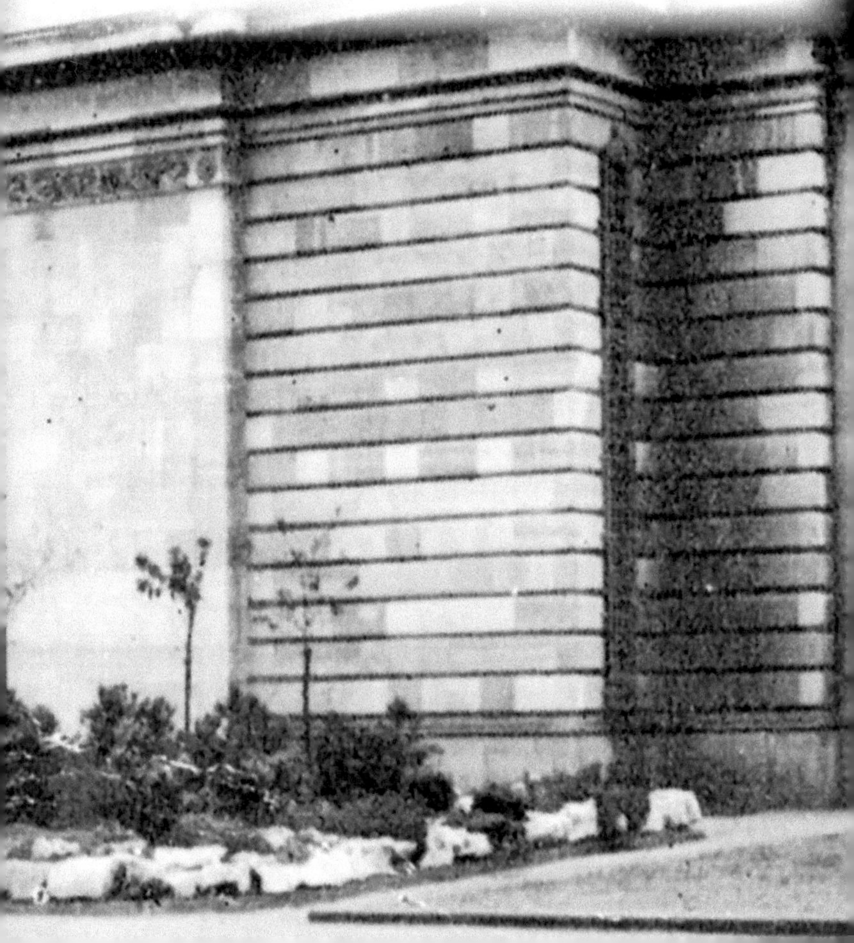

42. HALL OF MEMORY, BROAD STREET

This was built from Portland stone in 1923–24 in an octagonal form. Two of the four bronze statues can be seen; together the four representing Army, Navy, Air Force and Womens' services. Inside the structure is a hall, which contains a book of remembrance.

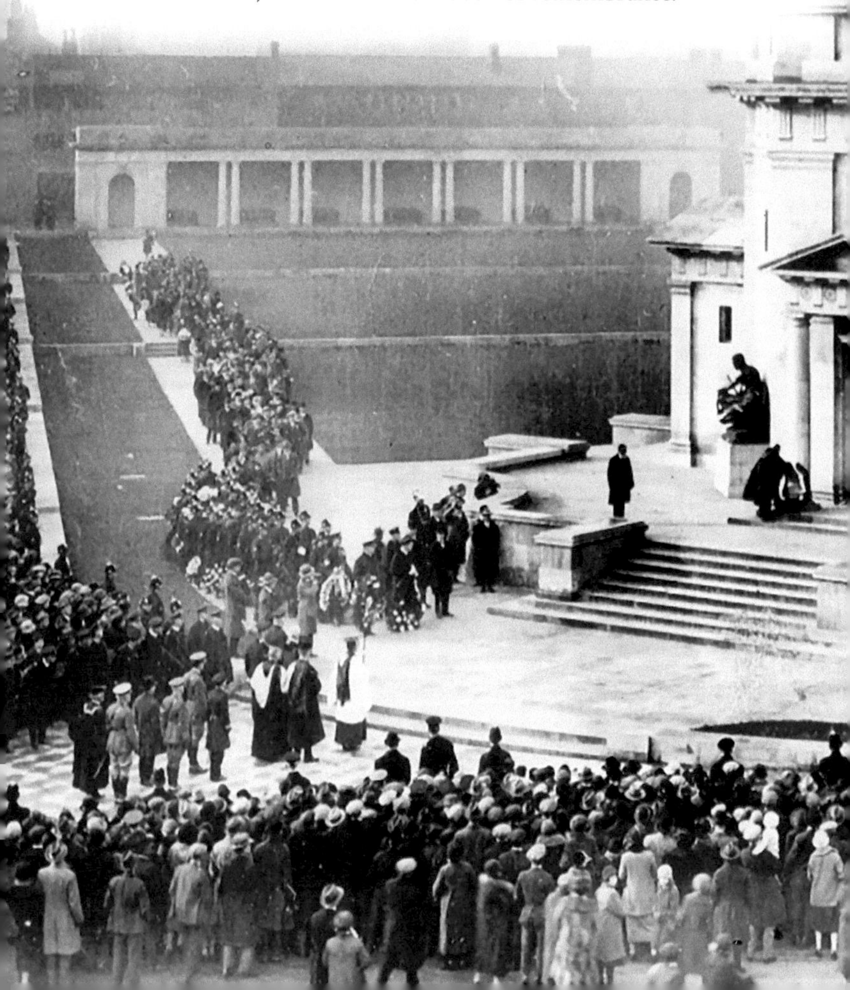

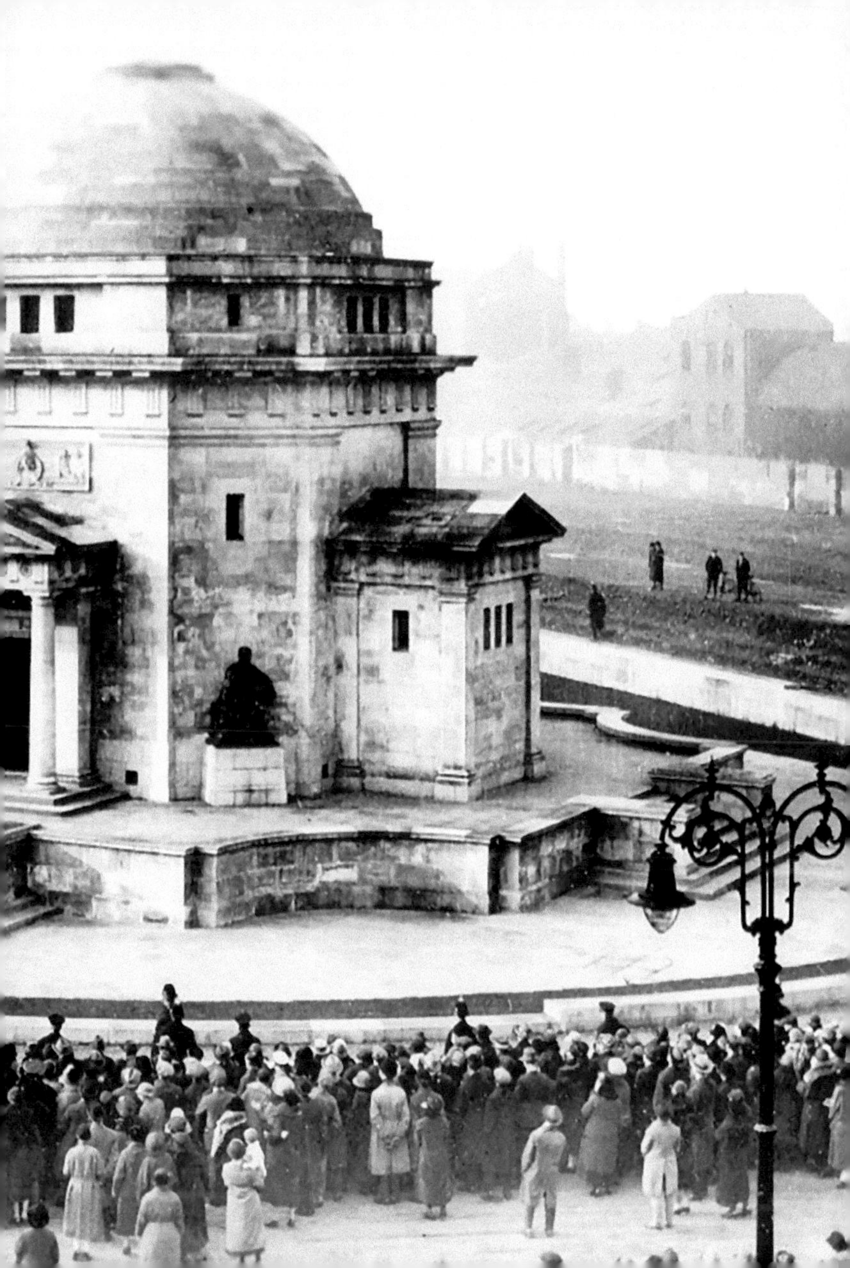

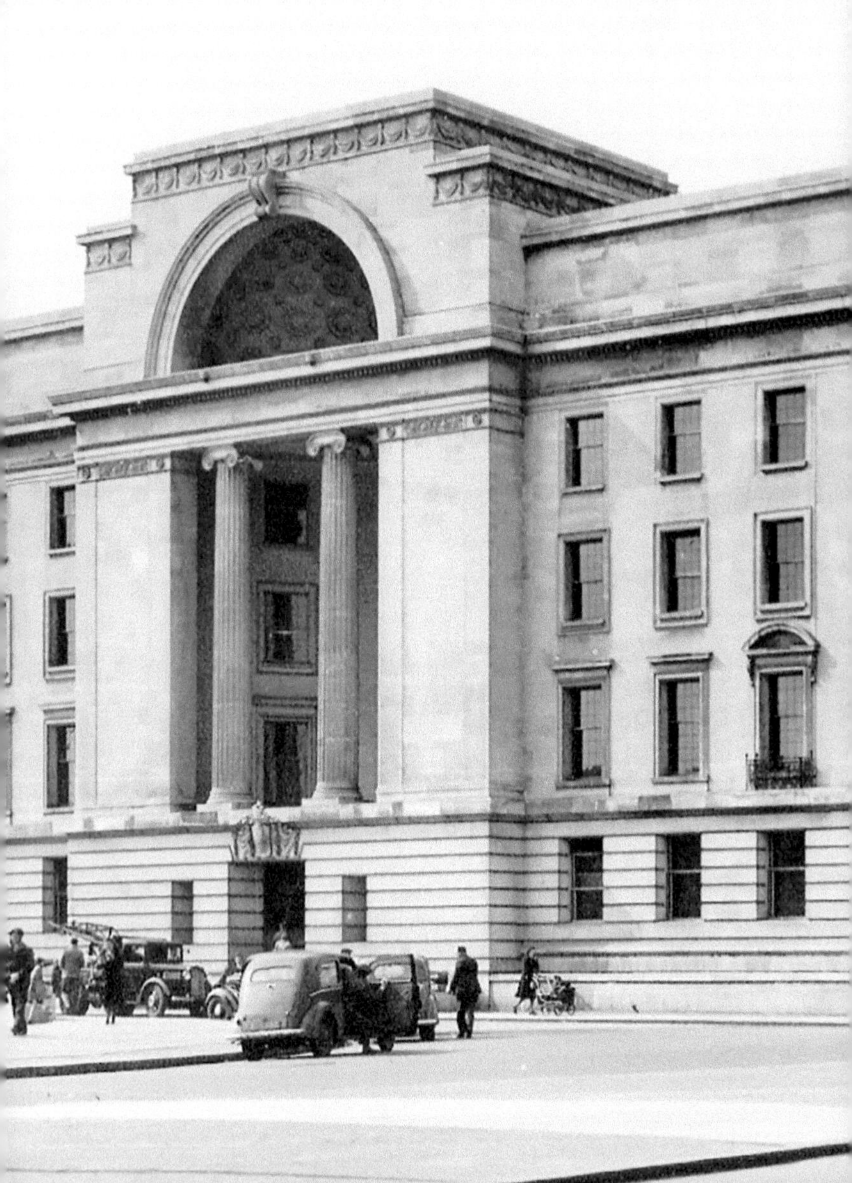

43. BASKERVILLE HOUSE, BROAD STREET

This building, named after the famous eighteenth-century printer, formed part of the 1930s 'grand design' for a new civic centre. It was hurriedly completed in 1939 and served as municipal offices. It has a grand entrance of iconic columns and high arch for the 'pen pushers' of the day.

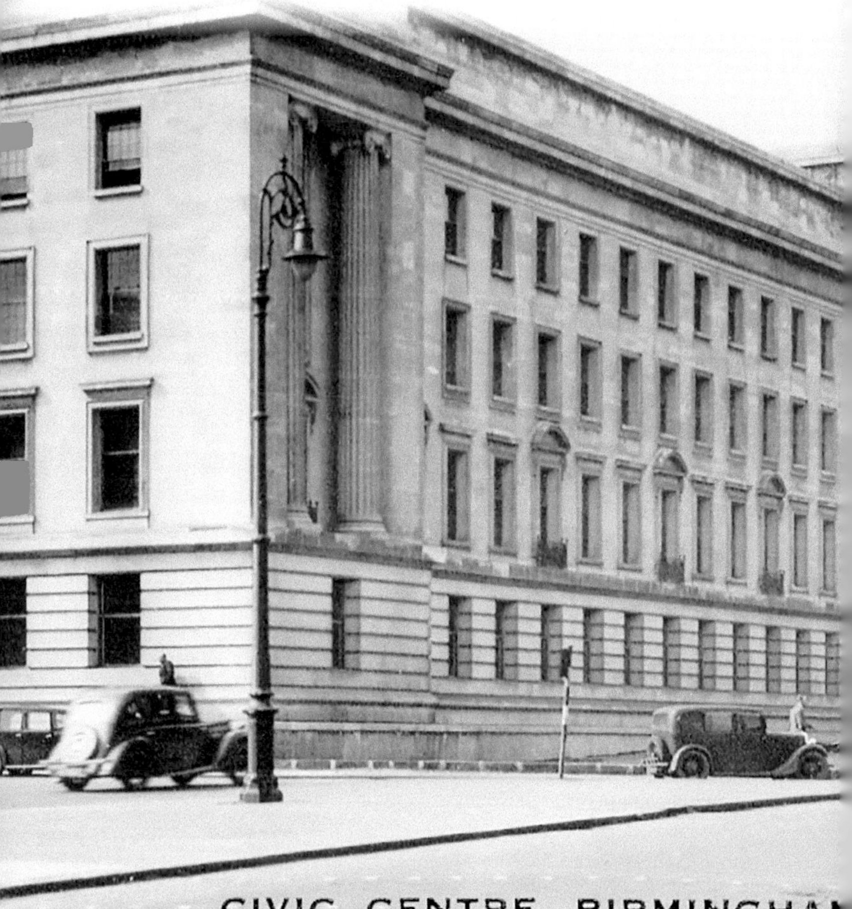

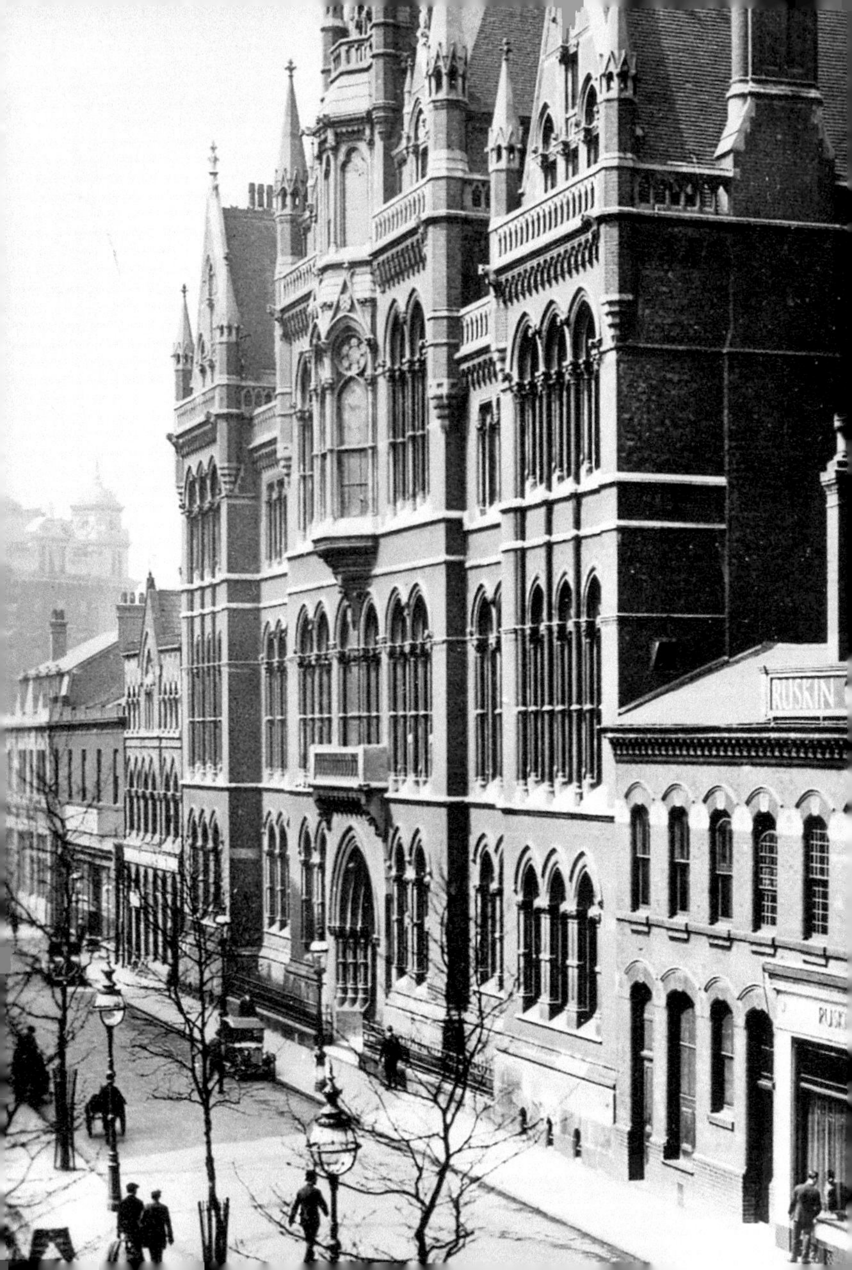
RUSKIN

44. THE UNIVERSITY, EDMUND STREET

Moving back along Broad Street, Edmund Street is soon reached. A college founded by a Birmingham philanthropist named Sir Josiah Mason opened here in 1880. The college was granted university status in 1900 and became part of the new red-brick university that opened at Edgbaston in 1909. This Gothic-style building remained home to the arts faculty until well after the end of the Second World War; it was demolished in 1963.

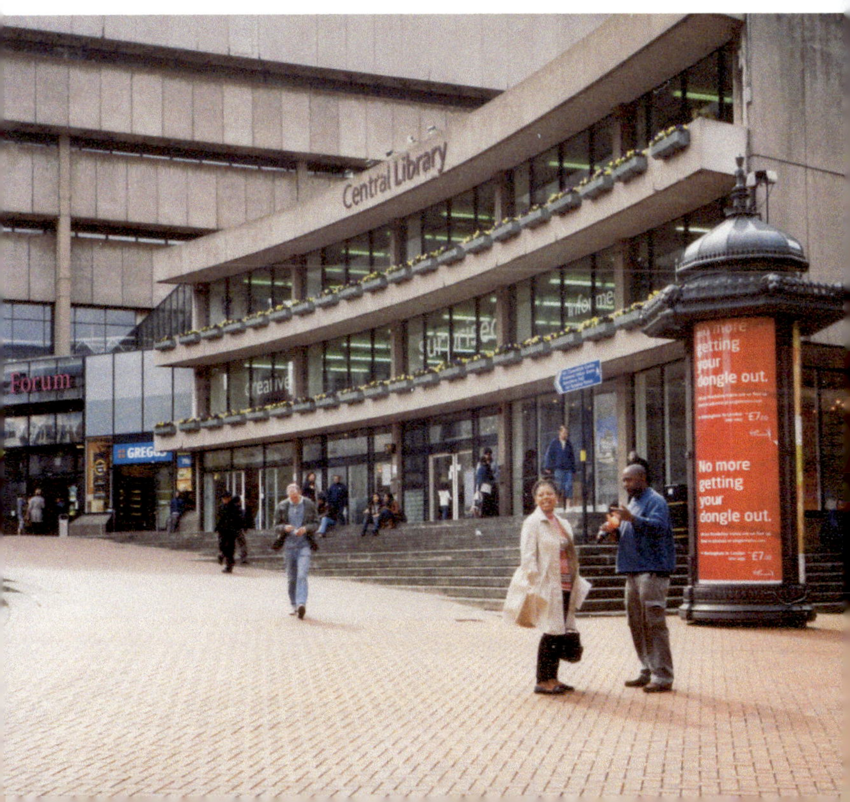

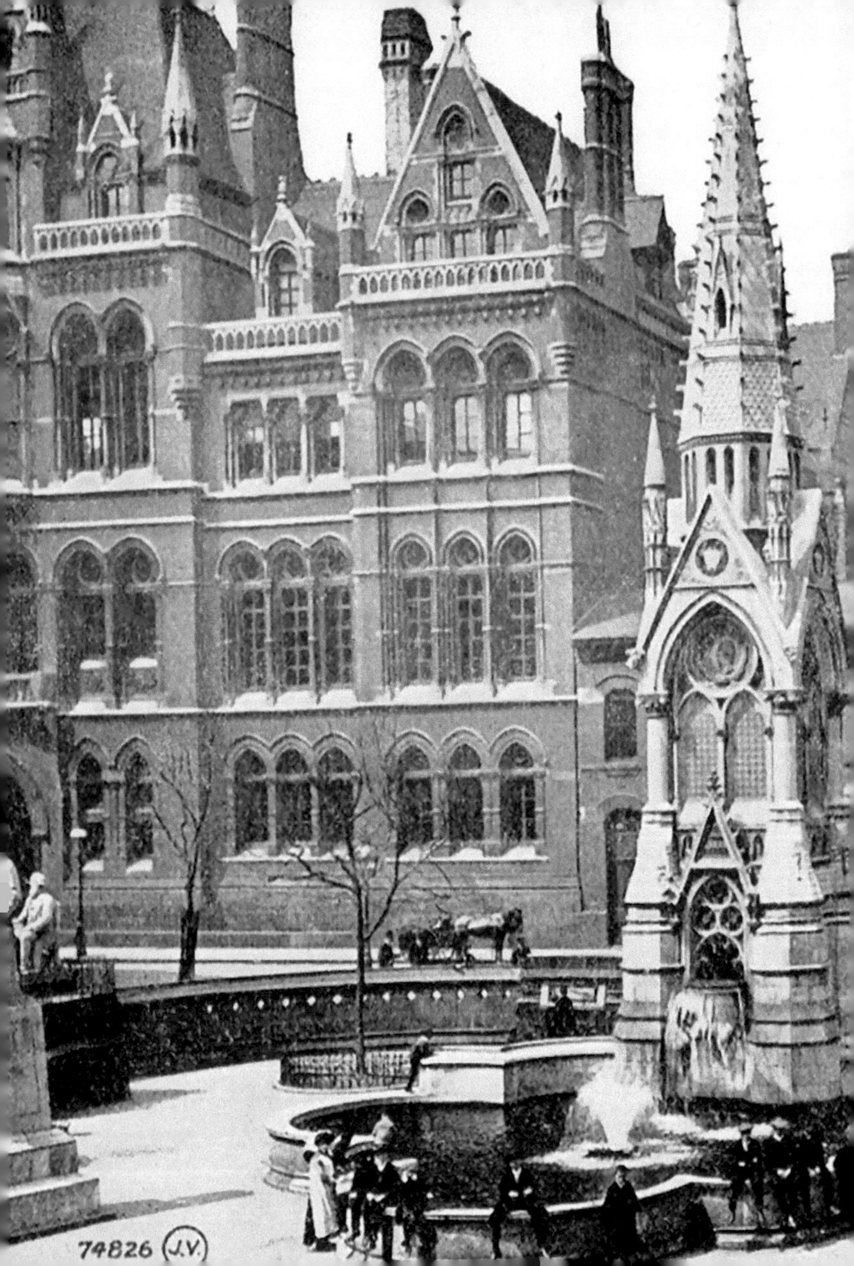

74826 (J.V.)

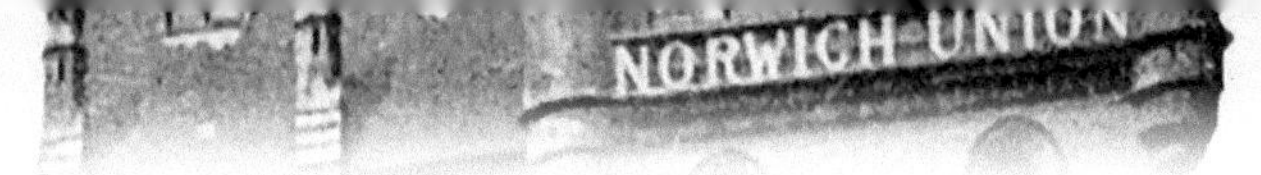

45. CHAMBERLAIN SQUARE

The university's neighbouring buildings form an interesting backdrop for Chamberlain Square, built to honour the city's greatest mayor and MP. A fair bit of clutter, popular at the time, was on show. The central memorial to the radical politician is, of course, the Fountain.

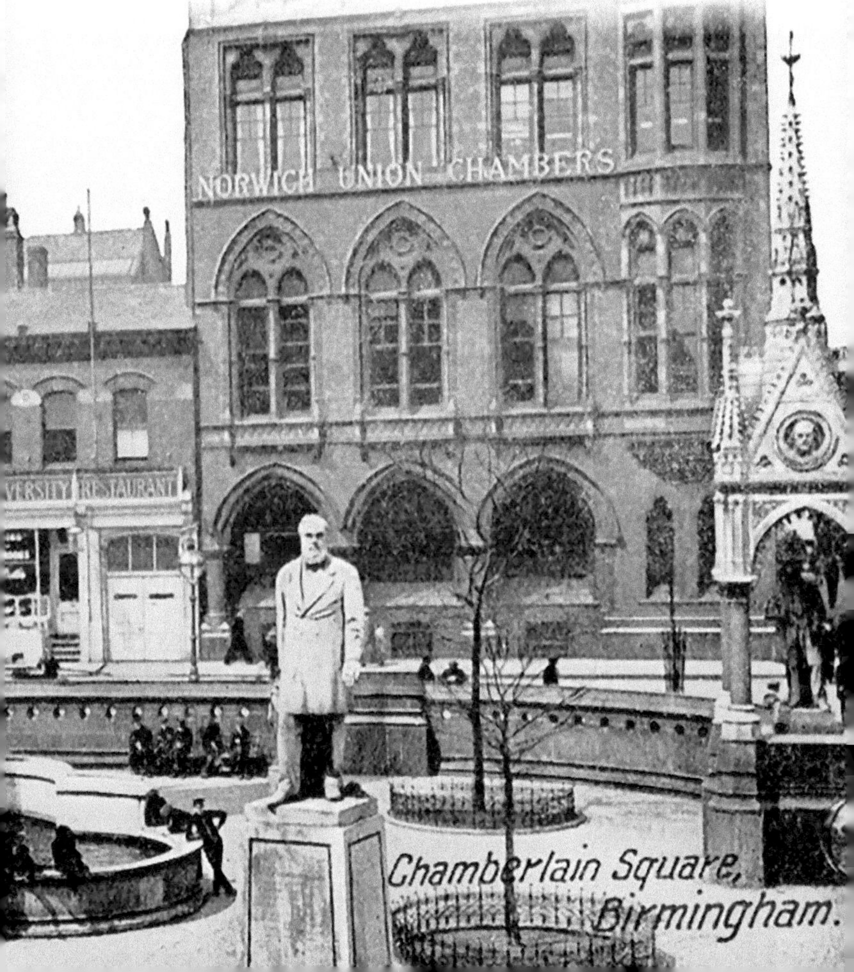

46. CENTRAL LIBRARY

Situated directly opposite Masons College University stood this fine domed building. It contained a large, spacious reference and reading room – a boon and treasure trove to students, research workers and the general public alike.

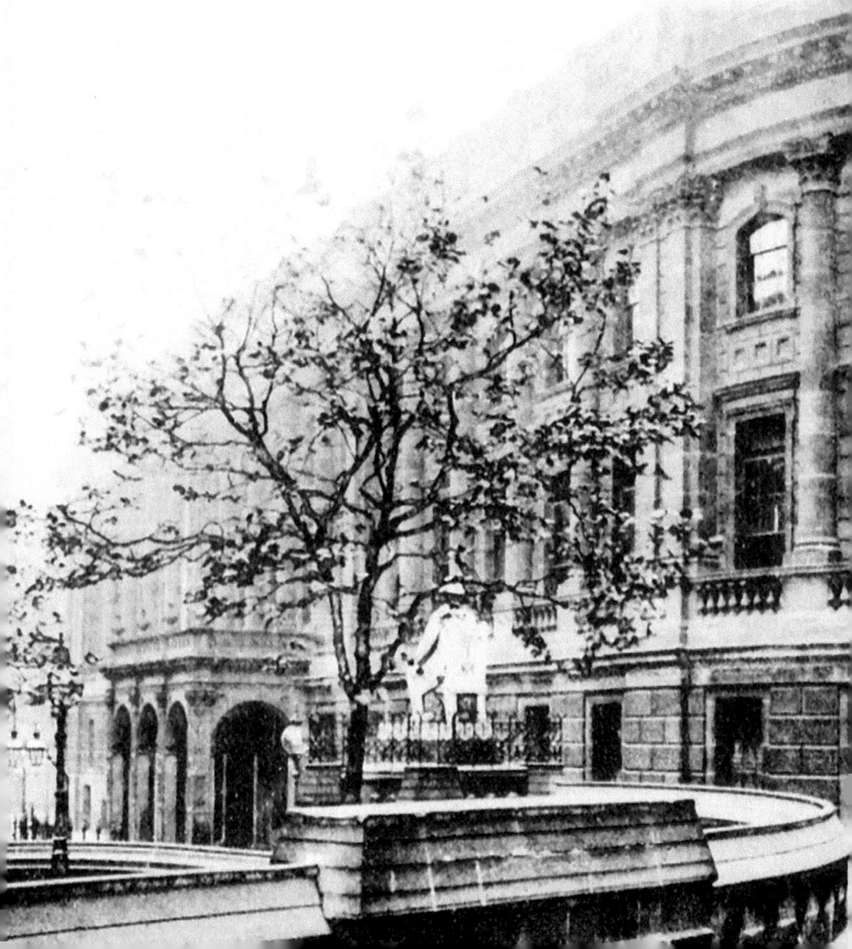

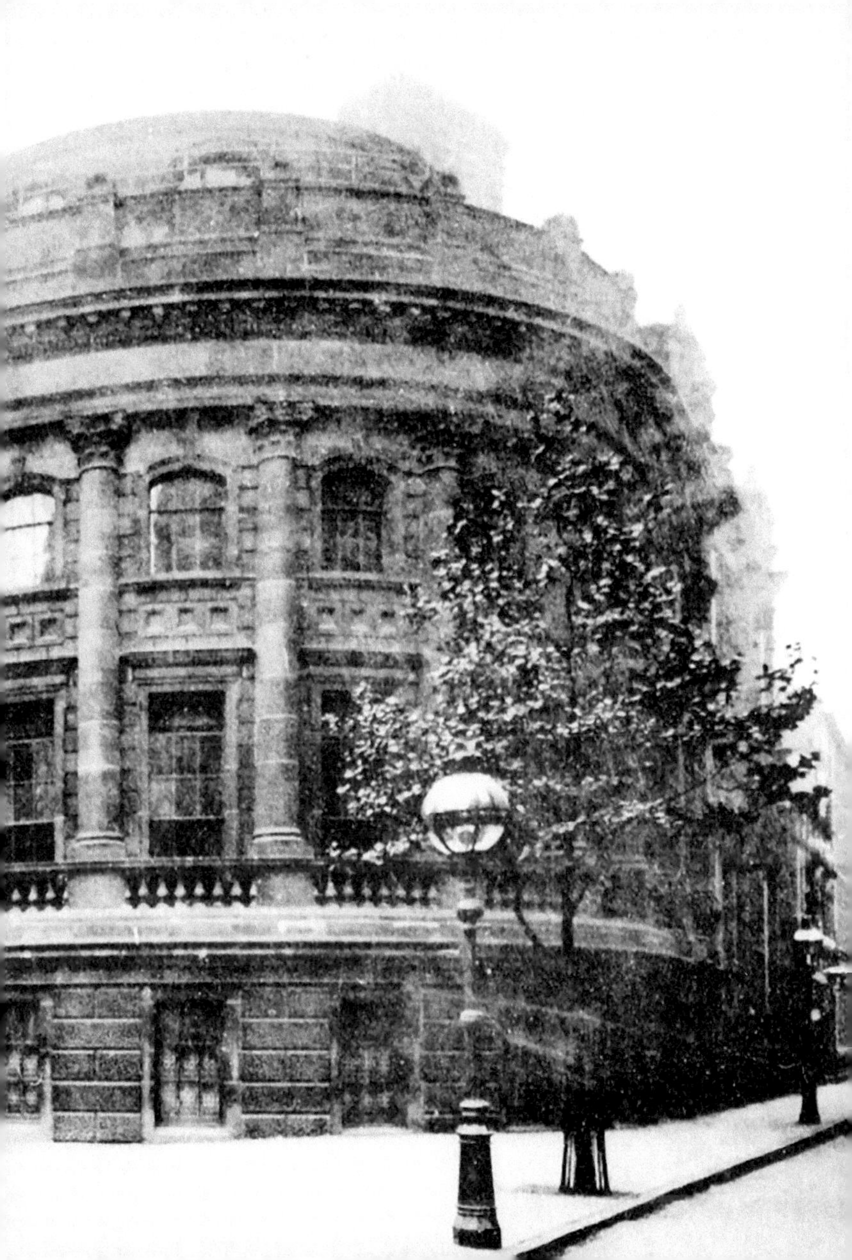

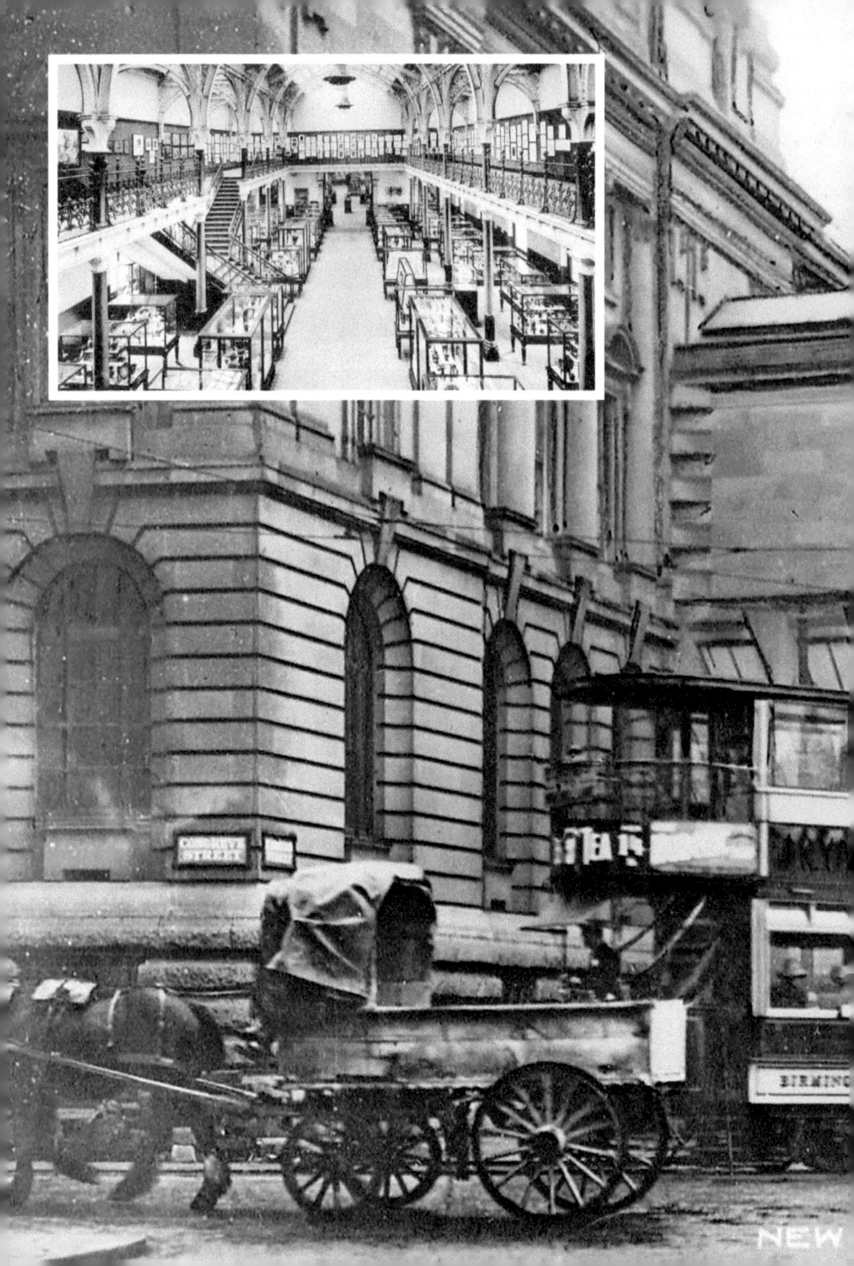

CONGREVE STREET
BIRMINGHAM
NEW

47. ART GALLERY MUSEUM

Bridging the gap between art and administration, this joins the gallery (on the left) to the council premises (on the right). Another tram terminus was here, this time with three routes. The tram shown is travelling to Cape Hill, Smethwick. The building of the museum/art gallery was constructed in the 1880s. Profits from the city-owned gas company founded the gallery and gifts in the form of paintings and porcelain were made by well-to-do business men. A major benefactor was Mr John Feeney, who bequeathed £50,000 – a significant sum of money in 1915.

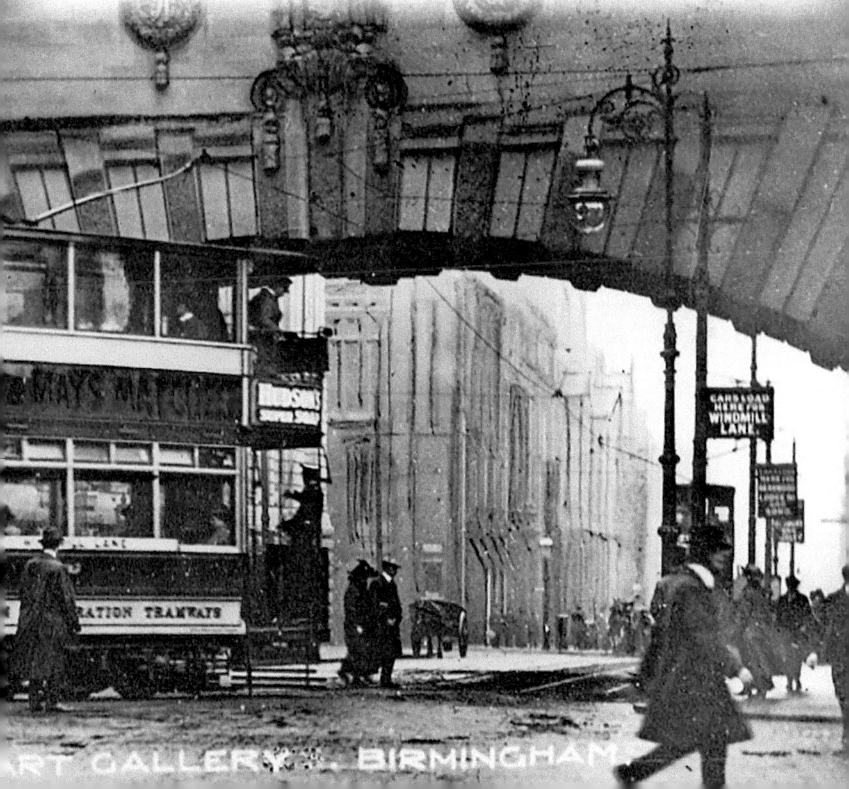

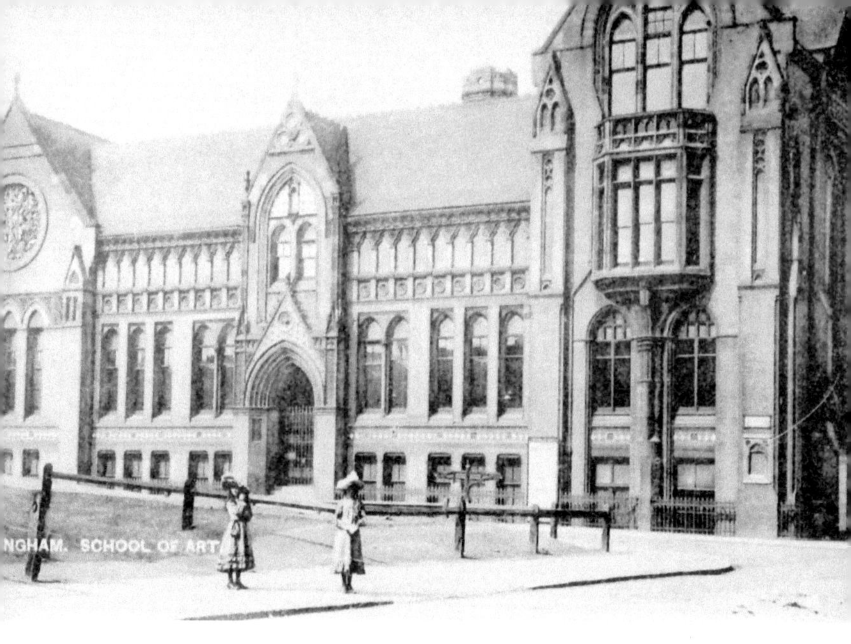

48. SCHOOL OF ART

Given the theme of the last few pages, it seems appropriate to end with a local artistic powerhouse. This fine building at the corner of Edmund Street and Margaret Street opened in 1894. With generous help from Louisa Anne Ryland, the first municipal art school came into being. It became a leader in the Arts and Crafts Movement and forms part of the new Birmingham City University.